IMAGES OF THE PAST

Holidays in

VICTORIAN

England

Margaret B. was an ordinary middle-class English girl of the late Victorian era, not wealthy, but comfortable. Her father was a Church of England cleric and, later, she would marry another.

Meanwhile, the family took holidays and made trips around England, not venturing abroad, and these are the pictures from those happy days, all sunny ones.

IMAGES OF THE PAST

Holidays in
VICTORIAN
England

GORDON THORBURN

First published in Great Britain in 2012 by
REMEMBER WHEN
an imprint of
Pen & Sword Books Ltd,
47 Church Street,
Barnsley,
South Yorkshire
S70 2AS

A CIP record for this book is available from the British Library.

ISBN 978 1 84468 129 7

Typeset by Chic Media Ltd

Printed and bound by CPI Group (UK) Ltd,
Croydon, CR0 4YY

Pen & Sword Books Ltd incorporates the Imprints of
Pen & Sword Aviation, Pen & Sword Maritime, Pen & Sword Military,
Wharncliffe Local History, Pen & Sword Select, Pen & Sword Military Classics,
Leo Cooper, Remember When, Seaforth Publishing and Frontline Publishing.

For a complete list of Pen & Sword titles please contact
Pen & Sword Books Limited
47 Church Street, Barnsley, South Yorkshire S70 2AS England
E-mail: enquiries@pen-and-sword.co.uk
Website: www.pen-and-sword.co.uk

Contents

Chapter One

Brighton, Lewes and the Downs

*D*eckchairs have not arrived in Brighton yet – note the benches on the beach – although they had been manufactured in Macclesfield since 1887. A hint of modernity in social standards, for which Brighton has always been noted, can be inferred from the row of bathing machines (upper centre left), considered surplus to modesty by the few brave souls dipping.

Like all the older seaside resorts, Brighton was a fishing village until fortune took a hand, in this case the famous dalliance of the then Prince of Wales, later George IV, with Mrs Fitzherbert. Fashionability was thus acquired, and the building of the

Pavilion in 1784-87 confirmed it, and Brighton's proximity to the Great Wen, a mere 50 miles on the London, Brighton and South Coast Railway after 1841, assured it for good.

This is the West Pier, opened in 1866. The bandstand (centre right) is fairly new at this point; the pavilion, built in 1893, is behind our view and the concert hall has not been added yet. The West Pier's rival, the Palace Pier, didn't open until 1899.

Regency Square can be seen where the pier ends, and the original Bedford Hotel, opened in 1829, destroyed by fire 1964, is the second building from the left, with the four columns. Where that stood, a supremely ugly monster was put up, to be taken later by Holiday Inn. In fact, little of our seafront view remains, mostly replaced by larger and less elegant buildings, as along much of the 4 miles of prom from Kemp Town to Hove.

Fire, storm, an aircraft crash and other disasters combined in more recent days to demolish West Pier almost completely, leaving an eerie island of steel marooned out to sea.

Beelzebub must have been a very busy fellow if all the valleys and earthworks called Devil's Dyke are truly his work. This one, an absolute must-see for all Victorian tourists in the Brighton area, was supposed to be the footprint of Satan, or hoofprint really, made when he turned up intending to stamp on the residents but got cold feet. Or, he was digging a ditch to let in the sea and was scared off by an old woman with a candle, or a cockerel, or something.

Another popular myth is that the Dyke was made by a glacier. It was made by a river, now gone, of melting snow towards the end of the last Ice Age, but remains one of the deepest valleys in the world that does not have a current river in it.

From 1887, visitors could take a train on a single-track line from Aldrington, Hove. From 1894, there was a cable-car across the valley, offering a ride about 100 yards up in the air. And then, from 1897, there was a funicular railway to the top of the valley. So, we know our main picture, with cable-car but without funicular, was taken between 1894 and '97, and we know that our young lady with the parasol (bottom right) had to walk it.

The cable-car is that dot in the sky centre left, with a lady and gentleman in it, with its metalwork tower on the right. In the enlargement we can see the man, amazingly, standing outside the car, perhaps seeking to impress his companion as young chaps are wont to do.

Out of shot, near the railway station, were fairground rides, bandstands and other amusements to cater for the many thousands who came, especially on public holidays to find that the Dyke was, well, just a dyke.

Apart from the hanging baskets and flowers in tubs, Anne of Cleves's House in Lewes looks the same today from the outside as you might expect of something built more than 400 years before our photograph was taken. The houses next door are the same too, although the yellow lines on the road are recent. It's now a museum full of interesting stuff from the time.

When Mrs Anne Tudor, the fourth of the eighth Henry's six wives, whom he called the Flanders Mare, was divorced in 1541, this fine house was part of the settlement. She never lived there, nor even went to look at it. There's another in Haverhill, Suffolk, and she never went to that one either. She liked a pot of ale and a hand at cards, so maybe she was happy at home.

The Lewes house is a fifteenth-century timber-framed Wealden hall house, which is to say it's a type of timber-framed house traditional in the south east of England, especially in the Kent Weald and east Sussex, built for one of the wealthier residents, possibly a wool merchant. The basic plan was four bays, with the two middle ones being open, making the hall with a hearth – no chimney at first – and the two end bays being reserved respectively for private life and food preparation. Later, chimneys were built, rooms divided and upper floors put in. The business end of the house had a buttery and a pantry; the private end had a parlour and a solar (sitting/work room for the lady of the house), with bedchambers above.

Originally, Anne of Cleves's House was thatched (note the steep pitch of the roof), with simple wattle and daub infill between the timbers to be limewashed annually. Later, the roof was tiled and the wattle and daub on the front replaced or faced with bricks.

Lewes goes back a very long way, being in the region of England where the earliest humans settled. It was an important market town and port in Saxon times, and when the Conqueror granted the whole business to William de Warenne in 1066, the first thing the new lord did was build a castle to guard the pass through the Downs made by the Sussex Ouse. He was quite a warrior, this William, fighting in Normandy before the invasion, at the Battle of Hastings, in the suppression of Hereward the Wake, and on King William Rufus's side in the barons' rebellion of 1088.

He died shortly after that, of wounds received, by which time he was the 1st Earl

of Surrey and a landowner in twelve counties. His castle in Lewes then was wooden; the stone version came later. William's bones and those of his wife, Gundrada, were unearthed in lead coffins during railway excavations in 1845, beside the Priory of St Pancras. Pancras of Rome, a fourteen-year-old martyr, is the patron saint of children rather than of railway stations.

There was also a Battle of Lewes in 1264, between insurgent barons (again) led by Simon de Montfort, and King Henry III. The King's son, Prince Edward, later Edward I Longshanks, was in the castle with the current de Warenne, John, 7th Earl, who at that moment was on the King's side, although he had been on the other. Anyway, de Montfort won, peace was made, and Lewes Castle and town went on to even greater prosperity.

When our visitors went, there were fairs five times a year, markets twice a week, and Harvey's brewery was already 100 years old.

Rottingdean, a few miles eastwards along the coast from Brighton, was also part of William de Warenne's empire, although in 1066 it was no more than a few poor farmers' hovels clustered around a pond. The original Saxon settler, Rota, gave the spot its name but very little happened after that until Brighton was on the up. The exceptions were the church to St Margaret (facing page), built in the thirteenth century, and the cricket club founded in 1758.

As Brighton flourished, a few of the more discerning visitors began looking for somewhere more refined, with less of the honky-tonk. Artists and literary figures found tranquillity here, including Sir Edward Coley Burne-Jones (Ned Jones to his friends).

An important part of any excursion to Rottingdean at this time, and now, come to that, was/is a viewing of the Burne-Jones stained glass windows, newly installed in the church in 1893 to mark the wedding of his daughter, also Margaret. The family had had a country house in the village since 1880. Ned died in 1898 and his ashes are in the churchyard.

The church looks much the same today as it did then, except the ivy is gone, there's a wall instead of a hedge on the right, the glasshouse is gone, and there's a porch over the entrance put up in 1909.

Another great attraction for the modern visitor is the restored Beacon windmill, built in 1802 but of no interest to our party because windmills were hardly a novelty and this one in particular hadn't worked for years. Perhaps our family would have dared to travel on the Brighton-Rottingdean seashore electric railway (see picture) but it wasn't open yet.

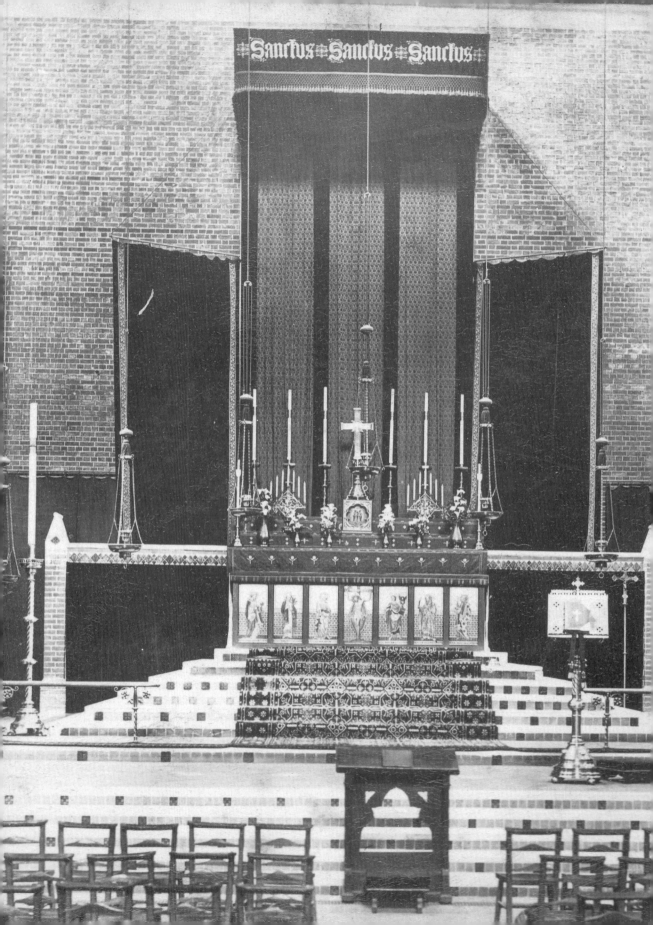

St Bartholomew's C of E church in Brighton is one of the tallest in Britain, not counting spires and towers, and was the first in Brighton (1874) to offer free admission to all of its 1,500 seats. Normal practice elsewhere was for the minister to collect fees from those who wished to reserve certain pews for themselves, while those who couldn't afford to pay, or who believed that all were equal in the eyes of the Lord, had to stand at the back. The minister behind the building of this church, Reverend Arthur Wagner, was a wealthy chap who maintained that salvation was for everyone.

When our visitors went to see it, the bricks were their original reddish colour, now aged to a blue-brown, and the roof had red and black tiles, now plain grey. The reredos and altar were as the picture, ornate by some tastes but not entirely out of tune with the rather plain, barn-like interior of the whole church.

This view has been spectacularly changed through works done after 1895 by a vicar who later converted to Roman Catholicism. A green and red marble canopy over the altar, white marble columns for candles, silver tabernacle, arts and crafts mosaics on the walls and other elaborate embellishments make our view unrecognisable.

Very little of all this pleased the traditionally minded Anglican burghers of Brighton. 'Cheese warehouse', 'Noah's Ark in brick' and 'uselessly large, painfully ugly' are a few of the choicer comments made about it. Coming into Brighton on the A23, you will see that it still dominates everything around.

Preston is a fully incorporated suburb of Brighton now, but it was a village in its own right on the London road and a church stood on the site of St Peter's – in the grounds of Preston Manor, next to Preston Park – when they wrote the Domesday Book. St Peter's itself is Early English style, thirteenth century, in flint with a tiled Sussex cap on the tower, like St Margaret's, Rottingdean.

The church overleaf had been extensively restored when our Margaret and family visited, with the ancient wall paintings revealed that had been plastered over during the Reformation, and it was still the parish church. The paintings they saw in all their thirteenth and fourteenth-century glory showed St Michael weighing souls at the Last Judgment, Thomas à Becket's murder in the cathedral, various saints, the Nativity and Mary Magdalene recognising the risen Christ. Such priceless pictures at a holy medieval exhibition can be seen today in the drawing by R.H. Nibbs (1851) but, alas, nowhere else.

After the railway station opened (1869) and the lord of the manor sold off a huge chunk of land for housing, poor little medieval St Peter's, capacity 250 of the

faithful, was struggling to cope and plans were laid for a new church, to be opened in 1902.

After a fire in 1906, which damaged the paintings beyond repair, parish status was changed to the new church, St John's, but the building of St Peter's was restored and carried on until 1988, when it was closed, then made redundant, then opened to the public as a curiosity of more than special interest.

PRESTON Church SUSSEX.

Chapter Two

The Day We Went to
Margate

'Kent is a maritime county, and one of the most beautiful districts in this island; it includes within its boundaries numerous objects replete with interest, and towns of high importance, magnitude and beauty.' When the editor of Pigot and Co's *British Atlas* was writing those words, in 1840, he was surely not thinking of Margate as a town of high importance and magnitude. It was still a liberty of Dover then, and no right of citizenship could be acquired until it was incorporated as a town in its own right in 1857.

Margate had been an obscure fishing village for most of its time, until around 1800, when it first became known as a bathing place and its many miles of sandy beaches began to attract Londoners. They came by steam packet and, after 1846, by railway. By the time this photograph was taken, around 1890, there were some thirty or so sailing boats taking trippers on pleasure cruises from harbour and beach.

There was a pier but it wasn't much of one, built in 1815 and used mainly by the local fishermen and the tramp steamers of coastal trade, and so, on a fine spring day (previous page), these late Victorians stroll along the prom, almost as many miles long as the beaches. A girl (low centre right) is being taken for a jolly by goat-powered cart, while two boys in sailor suits straddle an object replete with interest, a huge cannon, and imagine themselves far away. The gentleman on the end of the bench reads his paper, in front of the Ladies' Lavatories and, of course, there is not a motor car to be seen.

There are bathing decks (low centre) and a changing cabin/bathing machine, but no adults are wanting to be wheeled out into the cold German Sea, no matter how fine the weather. Two more bathing machines can just be seen below the cliffs (top centre) but again there are no takers today. Only children are willing to paddle in the shallow waters as the tide goes out, or search among the seaweed and rocks for crabs.

Most of the grown-ups prefer a gentle walk along the clifftop, towards the tearooms, while hardly anyone appears to be coming back. There are a few top hats among the gentlemen but the majority prefer a cap or boater for leisure wear. Many of the ladies have adopted the Mary Poppins look. Nobody goes bare-headed at any rate.

The Isle of Thanet, that most easterly part of Kent in which we find Margate, is in St Augustine Lathe. Lathes are unique to Kent; the name was used for the five administrative districts, from a Saxon word for land. St Augustine first came ashore here, at Ebbsfleet, when the Kingdom of Kent was a great power. King Aethelbert set him up in Canterbury (page 67) to fulfil his brief from the Pope: convert the Angles, the Saxons and, in Kent, the Jutes, to Christianity (success), and put the Celtic church under Rome's jurisdiction (failure).

The region was always one of the most productively cultivated and is still called the Garden of England, long after most of the hops, apples and cherries have gone but, this close to the sea, the fields are left to pasture. The onshore winds from the north east, bracing and refreshing as they might be to clifftop wanderers, are too much for young crops to bear.

Chapter Three

Buxton Spa and the
White Peak

—⁓—

*E*veryone's favourite view of Buxton, taken from the town hall, looking
down The Slopes onto The Crescent, is substantially the same today as it
was in Victorian times although some of the buildings have been put to
new uses.

The Crescent was built as an hotel for the gentry visiting the spa, became an
annexe to the Devonshire Royal Hospital, fell into disuse and decay and, after many
false starts, is now promised a refit as an hotel again.

The low building to the left of The Crescent is the Natural Baths, which became the Tourist Information Centre but now awaits development as the tourist spa and cosseting centre of the new hotel. To the left of that is part of the Old Hall Hotel, very ancient indeed, where Mary Queen of Scots is supposed to have plotted the downfall of Elizabeth I.

The building with the dome (138 feet inner diameter) was put up as stables and riding/exercise ring for the Duke of Devonshire in the late 1780s, without the dome originally but with its circular yard open to the sky. In 1859, roughly half of the premises was converted to a hospital, and the rest followed in 1881 when they constructed the dome, larger than that of St Paul's Cathedral in London and the same as St Peter's in Rome.

Gradually the requirements of a modern hospital became more and more difficult to sustain in the old place, and it fell empty too until the University of Derby took it on, refurbished it, and opened it as the classiest college anywhere in Britain for catering and hairdressing students.

With its back to us, flanked by two domed towers, is the New Pump Room, new because it was opened in 1894, replacing the old Well Room to provide elegant and peaceful surroundings for those wishing to take the waters as far away as possible from the hurly-burly of the charity patients, as seen in this cartoon from *Punch*, c.1885.

Not visible in the photograph but immediately to the right of the Pump Room, is St Anne's Well, from which, through a brass lion's mouth, pours a never-ending stream of the famous Buxton water, at a constant temperature of 82°F (27.5°C). The

spring water, having been underground for several thousand years, is exceptionally pure and was always available free of charge. Anybody can go with any amount of large containers and fill them, much to the irritation of those who happen to turn up just wanting a couple of bottles. The interesting fact that the water is free does not prevent many citizens of Buxton from buying it at normal bottled water prices in the supermarkets.

The Thermal Baths (far right) have their original glass and iron facade built in 1854, which was replaced by stonework in 1900. This is now a shopping arcade. To the right of that is the imposing terrace of shops and offices called The Quadrant.

Upper centre right is The Palace Hotel, opened in 1868 to accommodate the ever increasing numbers of folk arriving for spa holidays by train. It is still there and in business, the only one of the four such grand and immense palaces there used to be.

It's mostly students and commuters who arrive these days at the London and

North Western Railway station, beyond The Quadrant on the extreme right centre of the picture, sadly not in sufficient clarity (see enlargement, previous page) to see the Joseph Paxton window on the gable end. It was joined to the Midland Railway station, which was more or less identical, by a central gateway, part of which can just be made out. Both stations were opened on the same day, Saturday, 30 May 1863.

The picture gives the impression of a town built all at once, and that is not far from the truth, although what you are seeing is only the lower town. The fashionable popularity of spa treatments, of taking the waters and all the opportunities for what we now call networking, initially outstripped the local facilities. A furious surge of activity in the nineteenth century quickly put Buxton almost on a par with Bath, as it had been in Roman times when it was known as *Aquae Arnemetiae* (waters of Arnemetia, ancient British goddess of healing).

The church of St John the Baptist, Buxton, dated 1811, was built by the 5th and 6th Dukes of Devonshire with architect John White, in the neoclassical style in vogue in those Georgian times. It supplemented St Anne's chapel of 1625 (see page 26), which was too small to cope with the increasing numbers of visitors who, in those days, went to church every Sunday as a matter of course. Victorian holidays

included churchgoing and sightseeing visits to churches wherever one happened to be, on foot or by horse and cart (bottom right).

St John's could seat a thousand worshippers but, as a relic of its humble beginnings, Buxton was not a parish in its own right until 1898, previously being part of Bakewell. Even so, there seems to have been plenty of money about for religious donations. St John's marble and alabaster pulpit was paid for by subscription in 1867 as a memorial to the Right Reverend John Spencer, sometime Bishop of Madras and minister to the good people of Buxton.

The church contains a very fine organ and has legendary acoustic qualities that attract many musical events in modern times, and the church always features in the Buxton Festival.

The four stained glass windows by the star designer Charles Kempe would have been added by the time our holidaymakers went round.

Burials would still have been conducted then, but they were stopped by 1912, except for those families who already had vaults, because the water table – possibly influenced by the massive amount of new building all around – was discovered to be higher than previously imagined and there were concerns that bodies might rise up to the surface.

Saint Anne, or Hannah, as she would have been, mother of the Virgin Mary, is a shadowy figure. No question that Mary (Miriam) had a mother but there is no reliable evidence about her at all, much less that she was called Hannah. The story goes that she and her husband Joachim were childless and prayed to the Lord to end their barrenness, whereupon an angel came to call and blessed them, thus making history possible.

No mention in the Gospels supports this, and it is a retelling of the story of the conception of Samuel, so we have to conclude that scholars writing many years after the death of Jesus decided that the Son of God needed a grandmother.

Quite how St Anne became the patron saint of Buxton's springs is not clear, but all such springs were considered holy and each was placed under the protection of a saint. Thomas Cromwell, chief minister of Henry VIII, in seeking to destroy saintly influences, closed St Anne's Well after the Reformation but it soon opened again and has been popular ever since.

St Anne's small church was built in 1625 in the old town, the high part, the original Buxton with the London to Manchester road running through the middle. Beside that road functions the highest market in England twice a week, at 1,150 feet

above sea level (Alston in Cumbria is actually higher but there is no market there any more).

Had the photograph been of the original St Anne's chapel, there would have been crutches hanging around the walls, left there by penitents who had been cured of their ills by the waters and the saint combined. Alas, Tom Cromwell got rid of those too.

Four rivers rise by Axe Edge, a watershed around the 500 metre mark, and flow off in different directions. South-west goes the Dane, south-east the Dove on its way to Isaac Walton country and the beauty spots of Dovedale, east the Wye, which will become the Derwent for Derby, and north the Goyt, to more or less divide Derbyshire from Cheshire.

The photograph shows a wild natural scene, though industry is not far away. The Goyt is but a trickle here, not far from the Cat and Fiddle Inn; it gains strength passing through Goyt Moss, overlooked by Shining Tor, and heads for Whaley Bridge and Stockport, once powering many mills as it went. Goyt joined with Tame becomes the Mersey, in which it is united with the Dane, begun so close in the bogs of Axe Edge, and so to the Irish Sea.

Here we see the upper Goyt Valley; the road on the left, sweeping inwards, would place our photographer on the old Derbyshire Bridge, marking the boundary with Cheshire, and an easy walk from the dams below that now form the Errwood and Fernilee reservoirs. The shadowy fell in the background must be Wild Boar Clough, almost 550 metres. No sign, though, of the coal mining that for centuries fuelled the local lime kilns, but there are still remains of a great many mineshafts on Goyt Moss, top left of the picture.

The young man standing, looking coolly into the camera Cheshire side, perhaps one of our holidaymaking party, may have been interested to see the railway line that was then nearby, a goods-only route joining two canals that could go no further: the Peak Forest Canal in the west and the Cromford Canal in the east.

Waiting quietly in his light four-wheeler, posing for the photograph, our man with the white horse cannot have imagined what things would be like a hundred years hence, on the A623 Chapel-en-le-Frith to Baslow road, running through Middleton Dale, by the villages of Stoney Middleton and Eyam (see page 30). The folk of Stoney M left food for the self-barricaded Eyam villagers during the Great Plague.

Perhaps the carriage was our family's conveyance over the 10 miles or so from Buxton, via Miller's Dale (see page 32), or perhaps they took the train to Bakewell, bought a pudding for their lunch and hired the carriage from there. The three locals

visible in the enlargement, beside the track leading up to the limestone works, don't seem to be in a hurry either, although the standing man appears to be holding a small animal, possibly a lamb.

Limestone gives the district its name, the White Peak, a plateau cut in many places by river beds, some now dry. In this cut the Dale Brook still runs, and the modern quarries are behind us as we look. The slopes are rather more wooded now, and there are buildings and car parks for the quarriers. Otherwise our trippers would have looked over the same rolling grassland divided into small fields by drystone walls, the sheep, and the dairy cattle – a mix of traditional breeds and not the Holstein Fresians we see today.

Further north in the Dark Peak it was a different story, of privately held grouse moors on forbidding hills such as Kinder Scout and Bleak Low, not the sort of places for a genteel Victorian lady visitor to venture.

The view of Eyam's Church of St Lawrence has changed little. The ivy's gone, and a few of the gravestones. Two yew trees have grown but to the Anglo-Saxon cross (slightly right of centre) another hundred years and more has meant nothing. The cross, sometimes called the Celtic cross, is of uncertain date, carved between 650 AD and 800 AD, probably earlier in that period rather than later as it shows pagan as well as Christian symbols.

It certainly predates the church, which is mostly fourteenth century, although there are remnants of Saxon and Norman building, so obviously the cross wasn't made for here. Possibly it was a wayside marker originally, denoting a spot where the preacher would come at appointed hours to relay the messages of God. Anyway, it's not Celtic.

Eyam is always known as The Plague Village, with very good reason. In 1665, this killer disease was unknown in rural Derbyshire but it arrived in a bale of cloth ordered from London by a local tailor, George Viccars. The cloth, being damp, was laid out to dry, and Viccars was dead in days with some more who lived nearby. We know now that there must have been plague-carrying fleas in the bale, and a population of rats around the place for the fleas to live on, but in 1665 the villagers could only turn to William Mompesson, the rector, who asked them to quarantine themselves. Neighbouring villagers kept Eyam going with food left on the parish boundary. By October 1666, the plague had died out after killing at least the 260 people noted in the parish register but possibly many more. Mompesson's chair is still there, in the church that he closed to avoid assembly in a confined space. Wise man.

Miller's Dale (next page) was a busy place. Passengers changed at Miller's Dale for the Buxton branch line and caught trains bound for all stations to London and the north. Summer trippers by the thousand came from Derby, Sheffield and Manchester for a breath of fresh air.

The railway had transformed a rural idyll, where there had never been any industry beyond a few watermills grinding local corn. John Ruskin wrote: 'That valley where you might expect to catch sight of Pan, Apollo and the Muses, is now desecrated in order that a Buxton fool may be able to find himself in Bakewell at the end of twelve minutes, and vice-versa.'

With the railway came commercial cotton and timber mills, limestone quarries, and dairy farming on a much bigger scale now that hundreds of churns could be sent every morning to the bottling factories. Where there had been no village, one was built for railway folk, and the Railway pub went up (gone) and the Angler's Rest (still there), and the navvies built two massive viaducts from which modern trippers practise their abseiling.

The stunning beauty of the valley was spoiled for our visitors by industry, but not entirely so. Pan and the Muses were still imaginable, but probably not the great numbers of rainbow trout that now laze around in the river Wye as if they own it.

Then, the walk was along the old track in the bottom of the valley, from Cheedale to the wonderfully named Water-cum-Jolly Dale, with the railway above that is now part of the Monsal Trail.

Smaller dales run off north. Perhaps our wayfarers went up Monks Dale, all ancient woodland and wild flowers. Maybe the yellow spring cinquefoil was more common then.

Buxton is in a bowl, with hills all around, which accounts for every passing rain cloud always seeming to want to stop there. It also accounts for the gorges, the limestone ravines called dales that the river Wye has been forced to cut to find its way out of the bowl – or, as it was put in the *National Gazetteer* of 1868:

> Buxton is situated in a deep dell, in the midst of a hilly and moorland district, near the head of the small river Wye, a feeder of the Derwent, which flows through a deep ravine nearly parallel with

the high road leading to Bakewell. The neighbourhood of Buxton abounds in romantic scenery, steep rocks, wild chasms, wooded hills, with various and wide prospects. The cutting for the new line of railway is a very wonderful work, both on account of its tunnels and the height at which it has to be carried across roads and valleys at several points.

Ashwood Dale is the first dale and very wonderful cutting out of Buxton. In the photograph we see the Midland Railway heading for Miller's Dale, Longstone, Bakewell in twelve steamed minutes, and the whole of England and Scotland beyond. Just out of sight, top right, is the tunnel beneath Pig Tor. Nowadays the line then turns left up Great Rocks Dale to the quarries, for that is its only use now, as an occasional freight route for limestone.

Much more important to modern travellers is that little country lane, or 'high road leading to Bakewell', that you can see in the bottom centre of the picture beside the river Wye, which is the modern A6. Our picture appears to have been taken from Lovers Leap, a high point from which an entirely unknown number of lovers have leapt.

Prince John's Palace

Chapter Four

The Day We Went to Eltham

—✦—

When we say 'Prince John', we generally mean the one who became King John, signed the Magna Carta, failed to catch Robin Hood and was a Bad Thing. This is a different Prince John, and it wasn't really his palace at all, although that's how it was known locally.

He was born there in 1316, second son of Edward II and Isabella of France, only a few years after the building was finished and given by the Bishop of Durham to the King. John was made Earl of Cornwall at the age of twelve, commanded the English army in their victory over the Scots at Halidon Hill when aged seventeen and, at age twenty, had his bride chosen for him by elder brother Edward III. Alas, he died before they could get him to the church.

For another 200 years, Eltham Palace was a favoured royal residence, especially at Christmas and in the hunting season; the parks all around teemed with deer. The Great Hall (see picture) was commissioned by Edward IV, with a magnificent hammerbeam ceiling. Henry VIII grew up here, but the refurbished palace at Greenwich was more convenient by royal river taxi so Eltham fell out of favour and was wrecked during the Civil War.

The Great Hall was used as a barn for years but survived somehow, also a bridge over the moat and a strange house in the grounds (see page 36). The Hall was restored and incorporated in a new house in the 1930s by the Courtauld family, now a shrine to Art Deco.

We cannot identify our two young gents. The chap on the right poses elegantly, hat tilted but not, obviously, on purpose, while the one on the left puffs a huge pipe. The Victorian gatehouse beside which they stand is gone, replaced by a circular lawn.

Sir Thomas More's Cottage

Sir Thomas More's Cottage? It can't be, surely. It's not old enough. It looks like a suburban villa, nineteenth-century or later, except the pitch of the roof seems rather steep, as if it had been meant for thatch.

Ah, but, in the 1850s, somebody decided to clad the whole exterior of a Tudor timber-framed house with Kentish weatherboard, and put in new windows, and generally make what was known as Sir Thomas More's cottage, but which was really called the Chancellor's Lodgings, into something quite alien.

The picture is taken from the medieval bridge over the moat; the old buttery is visible on the right and the vegetation is moat-side.

What you can see today is nothing like it, because they took the weatherboards off in the 1950s and restored the original Chancellor's Lodgings to its oak and plaster, leaded window glory, adding another storey under the tiled roof with dormers.

Now, rather than the Victorian stockbroker's family our visitors might have imagined living there, we can see in our mind's eye the Lord Chancellors of the Tudor kings, Sir Thomas More among them, gratefully coming home to some peace after one of the King Henrys had been ranting all day about insufficient funds, or the trouble with Spain, and why things weren't so much better now that the Wars of the Roses were over.

In fact, it's four private properties today. Ordinary people live there. Let's hope they don't see Sir Thomas stalking the corridors with 'is 'ead tucked underneath 'is arm.

Chapter Five

Broadstairs and Herne Bay

—⁓—

The view over Viking Bay, Broadstairs, has not changed very much. Those in charge of such matters have, thankfully, largely resisted the temptations to which others in similar places have caved in. The building sticking up top right is Fort House, now much enlarged and known as Bleak House, where Charles Dickens wrote *David Copperfield*. He was a frequent visitor and got to know some of the locals, among whom was the lady he re-imagined as Betsy Trotwood.

The gentry had begun to arrive in the mid 1700s, in what was then a small and poor village. They built large residences, which must have deeply impressed the few hundred old Broadstairians who were, according to Daniel Defoe in 1723, ten per cent honest fisherfolk and the rest in the free trade, as smuggling was known. Such a story is told by writers and other non-residents about every seaside place in Britain, which makes one wonder how legitimate merchants could find enough business to make a living.

In Victorian times, as with Margate up the road, the holiday trade expanded at a terrific rate. By the time our visitors came to stay, the few hundred that Defoe counted had become 10,000, in Broadstairs and St Peter's, which was the inland settlement, originally more important, that was served by Broadstairs fishing.

It would seem that here, in September sun, bathers were more modest than those noted elsewhere, with the bathing machines in full use. In the detail, we can see many brave paddlers, fully dressed and behatted for the occasion, with mums equally in the fashion.

The jolly Jack Tar (one of Defoe's ten per cent, obviously) climbs up the jetty side while the owner of the photographer's studio scans the mud left by the tide. The young fellow in boater and plus-twos by the railings must be one of those poets or painters who found inspiration in Broadstairs, so deeply pensive is his pose, with massive book under arm as he gnaws worryingly at his little finger.

The purpose of the arch was as a gate in a city wall – to protect against invaders and allow friends. Indeed, it is called York Gate and was built in 1540 by one George Culmer to protect his shipyard, and to give citizens extra time to leave Thanet in case of invasion by Pope-inspired forces against Henry VIII. The threat, including a French fleet anchored off the coast, passed, and shipbuilding became important to the Broadstairs economy for 300 years.

The legend proclaims its creator and his date, and tells it was repaired (or repaird) by St John Henniker in 1795, doubtless at the behest of Broadstairs burghers who feared another invasion from France under the enemy's new Commander-in-Chief, Napoleon Bonaparte. The arch held firm but lost its *raison d'être* in 1824, when the shipbuilders upped sticks and moved to the Isle of Wight.

The tufts of weeds have gone and the arch has been restored, although the inscription is more weathered. The house on the right with the jettied bay window is still there. The flint houses on the left have become shops; the one above the arch was a dame-school at this time and is now an Italian restaurant.

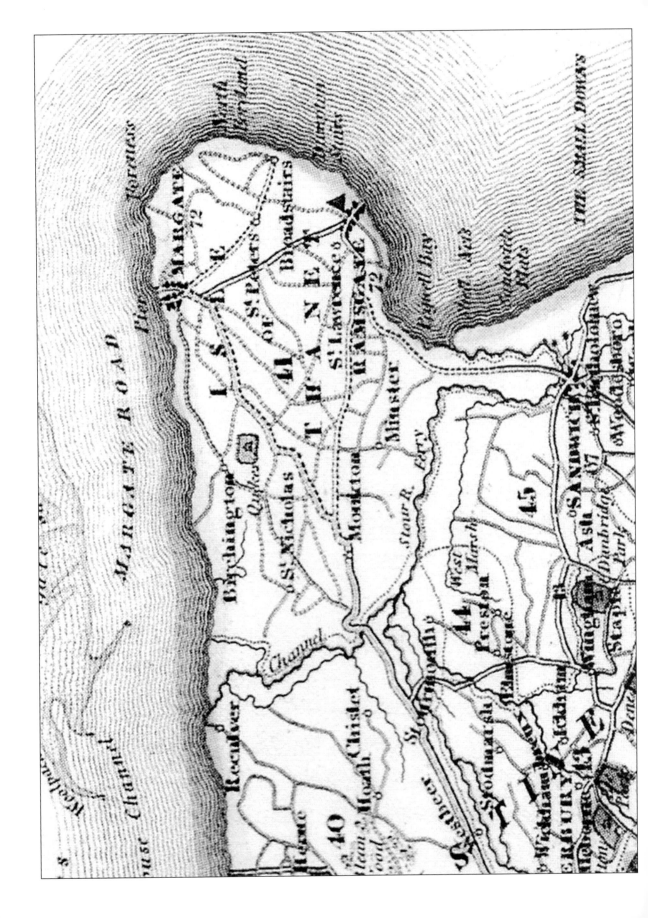

Minster was a village by the sea, at the mouth of the channel called the Wantsume that used to cut off the Isle of Thanet from the rest of Kent – see map for the two forks of the Stour, one flowing north to bog down near Reculver and one south, now bypassing Minster, looping down to Sandwich and back up to Pegwell Bay. This is all very important because otherwise we could not explain two saints, two semi-mythical chieftains and a lot of history.

The nearness of the port of Minster to the Continent was why the two chiefs of the Jutes, Hengist and Horsa, landed there, traditionally in 449 AD. It is not known if they were invited to help repel the marauding Picts, or if they sought sanctuary as refugees, but they and Jutish reinforcements did turn on their hosts and set up home at Minster, and eventually founded the Kingdom of Kent. You could argue, therefore, that as the first settlement of the pioneers of the great invasion by Jutes, Saxons and Angles, Minster was the first place in England.

Move on 250 years in this capital of Thanet and we find a princess of Kent, Ermenburga, founding the abbey at Minster and becoming a saint. Her daughter, Saint Mildred, became the second Abbess, and another princess (of Wessex), Saint Edburga, was the third Abbess. The abbey is still there, with nuns living in it as of old.

The Minster church of St Mary the Virgin (pictured overleaf) was founded in 670 AD by St Ermenburga. Her original wooden structure has long gone but we can identify the tower as Norman by its rounded arches, and behind the tree we can see Early English windows and door. The spire you see today is not this one, which was destroyed in the great gale of 1987.

44

The poser in this one, of the sea front at Herne Bay, is the fisherman, bottom left, puffing his pipe while holding his boat stationary. Otherwise it looks like a fairly quiet day when this resort was supposedly at its peak.

Herne Bay is almost entirely a Victorian invention. Before 1830 it was a small community with seagoing connections, a seaside suburb of Herne proper, then some London money-men built a wooden pier and a prom and the railway arrived. In ten years the population tripled to over 3,000, the first church went up, and Herne Bay was suddenly a tourist destination.

One visitor, a rich lady called Ann Thwaytes, so loved the place that she donated £4,000, an awful lot of money (about £2 million modern), to build a sight to see, which was the clock tower, left centre of the picture, 75 feet high or 82 feet including the weather vane, and thought to be the first free-standing example of such a thing in the world.

Steamboats brought more and more visitors from London and some of the fishermen turned to giving trips around the bay, in multi-purpose sailing boats called Thanet wherries, mostly built in Margate and more businesslike than the skiffs that crowd the shingle in our picture. A couple of these wherries are visible to the left of the clock.

Not in view is the new pier, under construction at this point to replace two previous ones. During the Second World War, sections of it were cut out so that invading Germans, landing on the end, would fall in the water on their way to the shore.

Reculver used to be at one end of the Wantsume channel (see map on page 42) and so was considered strategically important enough by the Romans for them to build a fort. The kings of Kent thought highly of it too and, as was their habit, set up a monastery. By Norman times Reculver was quite a city with perhaps a thousand people living there, but that was its high point.

As the Wantsume silted up and the sea eroded the cliffs, the population dwindled to maybe 300 by the time this picture was taken. Although there was a

brief revival in fortunes, now there is almost nothing left but the remains of the Saxon/Norman church.

That there are remains is no thanks to the incumbent clergy and parishioners of 1805, who set up a new church inland at Hillborough and knocked down the old one, leaving some rubble and the two towers, built in the 1100s, which had become navigation aids for shipping.

In 1810, Trinity House bought the towers. When a storm soon after that destroyed the spires, they put up the openwork structures with weather vanes on top, which you can see in the photograph. These have gone too, and the Reculver towers visible from Herne Bay are as fine as ever, but flat-topped and a little nearer the sea.

Funnily enough, the demolition job on the church turned Reculver into a visitor attraction. When the old pub, the Hoy and Anchor Inn, fell in the sea, another was built around 1830 and it's still there, thriving on hiker trade and the many caravan sites around on the clifftops, as the King Ethelbert.

Chapter Six

Folkstone

—⚬—

On the clifftop is that 'lawny level of inter-asphalted green' known as The Leas, with large boarding houses and hotels standing well back from the edge, broad promenades and grassy stretches lying between. Away to our left is the harbour pier; before us is the long pleasure pier, skating rink, switchback, in which children, and those who have the happy facility of becoming as children again in season of holiday, find varied attraction. On The Leas is a quiet promenade ... where on the level height the sea air may be enjoyed without any noise or disturbance from those who take their holiday more strenuously.

Thus spake Walter Jerrold in a Blackie and Sons' *Guide to Beautiful England*, writing at the time our pictures overleaf were taken. We know not which great poet coined 'inter-asphalted green', while Walter fails to mention the real point of The Leas: the view across the Channel to France. Proximity to France was key to Folkestone's change from fishing and trading port to top jumping-off point for Boulogne. The ferry business was huge; our family must have watched the steamships come and go, perhaps wishing they were a little better off and could afford to go abroad. The last steam packet sailed in 1980. Today there is only Eurotunnel.

Along with Faversham and Margate, Folkestone is a Cinque Port 'limb' of Dover, now an honorary matter but once serious business. Until Henry VII began building warships, the Cinque Ports had to supply most of the King's navy in return for privileges, mainly tax avoidance and self-government, also *infangenþeof* and *outfangenþeof* – the power to take a *þeof*, a thief, inside and outside the parish, and deal with him, which is to say, hang him.

The Victoria Pier, Folkestone, was opened in 1888, closed during the Second World War, became victim of an arson attack in 1945 that destroyed the pavilion end, and was finally demolished in 1954 by the Earl of Radnor's men. It was 683 feet long and there's nothing left.

Meanwhile, it was owned and run by various optimists. The original Folkestone Pier and Lift Company had high hopes of their floating landing stage for steamer traffic on the end of it, but nobody came. In 1892, the landing stage went, so we can date our picture after that.

According to the Folkestone and District Historical Society, the 'fine and commodious pavilion could seat 800 patrons and this was leased out to theatrical companies who provided suitable highbrow entertainments for Folkestone's largely aristocratic clientele. The pavilion held a six-day publican's licence and housed refreshment bars on the ground floor and a kitchen, dining room, bureau and balcony on the first floor.'

A little lower in the brow, possibly, the great Marie Lloyd also appeared there, and later Dan Leno, and Lily Langtry, who apparently was booed off the stage.

Our holidaymakers would have paid tuppence each to walk along the pier, something that was done by nowhere near enough people, according to our photographs here and on page 52 and the accounts of the FP&LC, which very seldom showed a profit. Perhaps there were too many aristocrats and insufficient young ladies of the ordinary sort who, according to custom and practice then, might accept an invitation from a would-be suitor to a turn along the pier as the opening sally in a holiday romance.

Folkestone's West Beach was the chief bathing area, mainly shingle with a sandy part near the pier. Later, the white sand East Beach, on the other side of the harbour, as it were behind us, superseded it but at this time the council hadn't yet cleared it of large rocks. Our section here in the pictures overleaf was for mixed bathing; further along it was ladies only.

The beach was owned by Lord Radnor, as indeed was most of the town, and you had to pay to go on it. If you wanted to swim in modesty, you had to pay again to use one of Fagg's Patent Safety Bathing Carriages. He had two, both in the picture. Presumably Mr Fagg was giving a rake-off to his lordship. If you preferred more privacy still, there were plenty of individual bathing machines.

In the enlargement, regrettably there appears to be nobody taking a header off the diving board but rather, we imagine, a school trip bathing without a risk assessment in the safety crate, under the supervision of Miss.

Perhaps when they come out, Miss will take her charges on the Victorian equivalent of the Big Dipper, the Switchback Railway, just visible in the main picture at the top of page 52 and in the enlargement below. This wooden white-knuckle ride was not motorised; it worked on gravity alone, and didn't work at all when the tide was in. Opened not long before our picture, it was badly damaged by storms in 1915, and demolished in 1918.

As at all seaside towns, there were pierrot shows and Punch & Judy, and trips around the bay. The sailing boat we can see – she is either *Maisie* or *Gertie* – took such trips, which looks more interesting than the modern equivalent. They knew

how to have fun in those days, as you can see from the expression on the boy's face, bottom right of top picture, page 52. Well, what would you feel like wearing a jacket, collar and tie on the beach? Maybe he wishes he could join in the game of Brolly Cricket being played centre left, although shingle does not make the ideal pitch.

It all looks terribly messy and complicated to our eyes, with these hats and big frocks, bathing huts, and almost horizontal, new and improved carriages on tram lines to be worked by hand, gas or other power (what other power – donkey?). The bather may be able to leave after taking his bath, without inconvenience of loss of time, but the moral and social standards of the period certainly made it hard work to be beside the seaside.

The Warren on the east side of Folkestone, here looking towards Abbot's Cliff and East Weir Bay, is the result of landslips in the white chalk. The photographer has carefully avoided sight of the Folkestone-Dover railway, hidden in the cleft to the right of the picture, and the Warren Halt, closed when this picture was taken after objections by the landowner, Lord Radnor. Perhaps our cameraman wanted to give us a hint of the railway, though, with the plume of smoke coming from an engine running along, up-centre right.

He has also given us the scale of his picture by placing that small boy on the ground, our poser for today (see enlargement).

Twenty years or so after our picture, anti-erosion measures were taken to protect

the railway, which had the additional benefit of keeping The Warren more stable. There are still rockfalls but the view remains pretty much the same, and it's a Site of Special Scientific Interest. A modern photographer wishing to give an entirely tranquil view would have little trouble emulating our Victorian and, of course, would not be bothered by steam.

For the scientifically minded, the cliffs are Cretaceous period, around 150 million years old. Fossil hunters on the beach, which is denuded of sand in the winter to expose the Gault clay, may be very lucky and find a piece of plesiosaurus. Or, as the British Geological Survey puts it, 'The Folkestone Warren landslide is one of the largest on the English coast and is a classical example of a deep-seated multiple regressive, compound mechanism, having translational, rotational, and graben features.' And you can't say fairer than that.

The first church in Folkestone and the only one for many centuries was (and is) dedicated to local girl, St Eanswythe. Her grandfather was King of Kent, Æðelbryht (the shining noble one, now usually spelled Ethelbert), a Christian convert and headed for sainthood too. The bad news was her father, King Eadbald (the happy bold one) – a pagan.

Eanswythe (the marvellous lamb) was brought up a Christian by her mother,

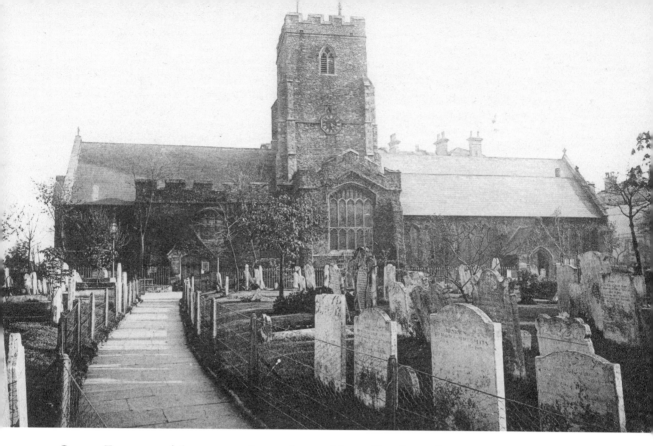

Queen Emma, and from an early age devoted herself to her religion. The story goes that father wanted her to marry a Northumbrian king but she wasn't keen, one, because he was a pagan and, two, possibly, because things were ever in a turmoil up north. Kings there tended to live active but short lives, ending on the battlefield.

Fitting the timing is King Edwin, in which case there was a third objection. He was already married. Later he turned Christian, was slain in 633 and made a saint, but Eanswythe saw only a heathen warlord. She stood up to her father, setting Edwin, if it was he, a task.

Work had begun on the first nunnery in Britain, at Folkestone, which Eadbald was building for his wayward daughter. One of the structural beams was too short, so Eanswythe asked Edwin if his gods could intervene to lengthen the beam.

Not surprisingly, seeing as those gods would not be enthusiastic about lengthening beams for a Christian nunnery, Edwin failed. Eanswythe said a little prayer and lo, the beam grew. Edwin went back to Tyneside in shame.

Water for the nunnery had to be carried a mile, so Eanswythe went to the spring with a magic wand and bade the water follow her to where she wanted it, whence it sprung in abundance. Other miracles were more usual, such as casting out devils, giving sight to the blind, and telling the birds not to eat the newly sown corn in the nunnery fields.

Eanswythe died in 640 AD, aged twenty-six. Her church was pillaged by Vikings or maybe fell in the sea. Another was built by King Æthelstan (the noble rock) in 927, but that didn't last either. After the Norman invasion, Nigel de Muneville founded a priory on the cliffs, which also threatened to fall in the sea by 1138. A new one was dedicated to St Mary and St Eanswythe, which formed the foundations of the church we see now, even though it burned down in 1216, was rebuilt in 1220 and was extended in 1236. Those last alterations included the Early English east window at the altar (see picture page 56).

More improvements and partial ruinations followed, until a half century of restoration and adornment began in 1859, all in the high church tradition and mostly in the photo, although not all there today. St Eanswythe's relics somehow survived and still lie behind the door under the mosaic of St Peter.

They have Town Sunday in Folkestone, but it's not as good as it used to be. In the old days, everyone came to the churchyard when a horn was blown, to elect the mayor. A charter from Edward II said they could have a mayor, so they would, and the chosen fellow usually agreed because, if he didn't, the people could pull his house down. Now they just have a normal election, followed by prayers in the church of Saint Eanswythe.

Chapter Seven

The Day We Went to Aylesford

—⚏—

Aylesford is all about the river, the Medway, tidal to this point and a few miles beyond. There are Stone Age, Bronze Age, Iron Age and Roman remains, all because of the importance of the low-tide river crossing. There may have been a Romans v Britons battle here, and there was a Jutes v Britons one, when our friends Hengist and Horsa fought the natives, possibly under their King Vortigern, in 455. Horsa was killed and, after another battle or two, Hengist made himself King of Kent.

Two or three hundred years after that, a fellow of rank called Ægel set up a farmstead and small community at the crossing and gave his name to it:

Ægelesforda. In the fourteenth century they built the bridge you see in the picture, initially with small arches all the way across; the central arch was made later, to accommodate the increasingly busy river traffic. It was the first bridge after Rochester, upstream 12 miles, and it still was until 1963.

Aylesford and several other villages had wharves for loading the flat-bottomed sailing barges. We can see a cartload of grain in mid-tip, with carter's boy and horse holding steady for the camera. The old chap on the bench looks up from his lunch. Maybe he bought a pie from the grocer's shop, or possibly some of that Fry's Chocolate to make a cup for a luxury breakfast tomorrow. Or not.

The old houses are still there, and the wharf. Take away the sailing barges and the view is not much altered, except the bridge is now pedestrians only and there's a new bridge further along, not to mention motorway viaducts. Ægel his ford is not quite so important as it was.

Chapter Eight

Hastings

—⁂—

Hastings Castle had nothing to do with the battle of 1066. A wooden structure, thrown up on the orders of William the Conqueror, might conceivably have seen action if the said battle had been lost and William had had to retreat, but he didn't. While the rest of the town prospered greatly as one of the Cinque Ports, the history of Hastings castle was unexciting.

The Conqueror ordered a stone rebuild in 1070 and gave Hastings to Robert, Count of Eu (an area of northern Normandy), who had fought with him in the conquest in question. When William died and his son William Rufus succeeded,

Robert's son and heir, another William, rebelled, lost, took trial by battle, lost again and suffered the usual punishment, which was blinding and castration. He died of it, but a long way from his castle, in Salisbury, in fact, and his son Henry succeeded to the family fortune.

Nothing much happened for the next hundred years or so, until King John ordered the castle to be pulled down in case the French should take it, which seems to be missing the point somewhat, but Henry III had it put back up again.

That was in 1220. In 1287, a long-lasting series of storms caused a massive cliff fall and parts of the castle went over the edge. More went later, and you can see what was left by the time our visitors looked round.

Although the Germans caused more damage in the Second World War, this view remains much the same. It's the only full archway still standing. Curiously, in our picture there is no poser, not even a small boy hiding in the ivy, which, incidentally, has all been removed.

At the end of Rock-a-Nore road, to the east of Hastings Old Town, the wild coast begins. The railings in the picture, bottom left, now prevent bird-watchers' four-wheel drives from plunging into the sea, but at our time there was no such thing as a car park. Behind us is the harbour and the Stade – the shingle beach that is now

home to the largest fleet of shore-launched fishing boats in Europe – and the tall, black, wooden 'net shops' for storing fishing gear (not for drying nets, as commonly thought).

Groynes like the one you can see are there to stop sideways shingle migration. They were mostly put up in Victorian times when the Stade was much smaller and the fishermen fewer, and their boats had to be hauled up the beach by capstan and horse.

Many years ago, this would have been part of a river delta, with sediments being laid down ready to be trodden in by dinosaurs. Assuming it was a sunny day, the mud would dry and harden. Then, next time there was heavy rain and the rivers in the delta overflowed, the footprints would be filled by a different sediment.

After waiting for 150 million years, and a few more hours for the storm to abate and the tide to go out, our Victorians could search among the rocks for very large three-toed footprints, without the benefit of modern science to say exactly what they were. The sandstone cliffs have always been unstable and rockfalls frequent, so a boulder on the head could be the price paid by the unwary trophy hunter, but this was (and is) one of the very few places in Britain where such fossilised excitement could be had.

Ecclesbourne Glen (with the bridge) and Fairlight Glen (overleaf) are now part of

the Hastings Country Park Nature Reserve, which in turn is part of the High Weald Area of Outstanding Natural Beauty. The glens are more properly called gills, and their ancient woodland is home to rare wildlife not found elsewhere in south-east England, requiring a humid, frost-free environment that these steep-sided valleys provide.

We don't know if our Victorians were able to identify scarce bryophytes (mosses and liverworts) and diptera (two-winged flies) or, indeed, the very rare money spider *Diplocephalus protuberans*. The dormice that live here were not so unusual then, so they might have hoped to spot one of those.

There are car parks now but our visitors would have had to walk and, after making all that effort, would surely have gone down to the beach to see the stream from Ecclesbourne Glen ending in a waterfall. If they managed the old path down to the beach at Fairlight, they would certainly not have been greeted by its modern users, the local naturists.

Chapter Nine

The Day We Went to Faversham

—⋙—

At the time of this picture overleaf featuring the splendid Guildhall, Faversham was described as a market town and river port, member of the Cinque Ports of Dover, on a creek of the river Swale and on the Southern Railway. Population was about 11,000, working in the hop fields, the cherry orchards, the Shepherd Neame, Fremlins and Whitbread breweries, the gunpowder factory, in the shipping trade and on the oyster beds, managed by the Company and Fraternity of Free Dredgermen of the Hundred and Manor of Faversham.

This Company was for married men only and had been going strong since the

twelfth century. When our visitors came for their day, whispers of trouble could be heard in pubs like the Bear Inn on the left of the picture and the New Inn on the right. The council had taken the easy way with the rapidly expanding sewage problem and had the lot discharged right into the river. By 1903, the oysters were declared unfit. Although a proper sewage system was installed later, the oyster beds never recovered properly and eventually failed entirely.

So, no Faversham oysters for the modern visitor, and no pint at the New Inn either. It's gone. Note our poser who, apart from his apron, has kept still for long enough, while the dog would not stay and the two workmen have become four, perhaps discussing what to do with the sign for T.P. Hissey, Clothier.

Messrs Carter and Webb have pulled down the blinds on their display of clocks and watches. Their shop has been replaced by a faux-Tudor estate agent's but many of the medieval buildings remain, thanks to a win for the citizens against the planners.

Chapter Ten

Canterbury

—⚹—

Canterbury Cathedral? Archbishop of Canterbury? Metropolis of the Christian church in England and the centre of the Anglian Christian world? It all began with a ford over a river in the Stone Age.

Routes to and from the coast and important places further north, converged at the ford over the Stour. A settlement grew up, which gradually became the natural capital of the local British, the Cantiaci. The Romans came, built the town larger and stronger, abandoned it, then the Jutes turned up (see above) and colonised the place, naming it *Cantwara burg*, the fortified place of the inhabitants of Kent.

Top status was confirmed when King Æðelbryht made it his capital. His queen, Berhta, Berþa or Bertha, was already a Christian and so, when Saint Augustine landed, he called on the royal family, converted them, looked about him and saw the obviously ideal spot for his holy headquarters. Berþa and Æðelbryht provided the means for an abbey, wherein Augustine could have his cathedra, or chair, and a church, St Martin's (page 72 top right and page 73).

One of the more important things to happen to the city after that was the influx, in the time of Queen Elizabeth I, of persecuted Walloon Protestants from France and the Low Countries, called Huguenots. They brought with them their industry of silk weaving, which became Canterbury's premier pursuit after pilgrimages, one of the results of which was our picture overleaf. Today, what are known locally as the Huguenot weavers' houses, overlooking the river are much restored and sport hanging baskets of flowers. So, you can see a view like this one, if not quite so endearingly seedy, despite severe damage in the air raid of June 1942.

According to the Anglo-Saxon Chronicle for 754, *Cantawara forbærn ðy geare* – Canterbury was burned in that year, and the town was *bræcon* – broken, taken by force – in 853. Kentish history is very obscure in this period, but these disasters were probably the result of struggles for the throne – there often seem to have been several kings of Kent at once – and clashes with rival kingdoms, particularly Mercia.

Saint Augustine's original monastery was mended and enlarged, but burned down in 1067, one year after the Norman invasion (which Kent did not resist) and was completely rebuilt, starting in 1070, set back again by fire in 1174, completed in 1184, with major additions in 1376, and c.1495, the central tower was put up. The interior view towards the quire in our picture overleaf has changed only a little; the screen in the centre has gone.

The making of Canterbury as a thriving and wealthy city was given a massive boost when Archbishop Thomas Becket was murdered in the cathedral in 1170, canonised in 1172, and awarded a magnificent shrine in the rebuild of 1174. Immediately miracles occurred, wars were won and, as Geoffrey Chaucer put it, people could have help when that they were sick.

Thanne longen folk to goon on pilgrimages ...
And specially, from every shires ende
Of Engelond, to Caunturbury they wende,
The hooly blisful martir for to seke,
That hem hath holpen whan that they were seeke.

The Abbey of St Augustine was founded partly to provide a suitable resting place for the remains of the kings of Kent and the archbishops of Canterbury. As it turned out, not many of them ended up there. Our friends King Eadbald and Queen Emma did, and Saint Justus, the fourth archbishop, but other options proved more popular.

The Normans didn't think much of the Saxon buildings and soon had their own style imposed, so that only a few traces are left of the original beneath their heavy, round-arched masonry. By 1500, the abbey was a huge institution with a library of 2,000 books, an enormous number for the time, and its size saved it from Henry VIII's first round of wreckings of 1535. He set an income threshold of £1,000 a year, below which all monasteries would be closed. This abbey had £1,733. The reprieve lasted three years only; dismantling began, although part was kept as a college with fifty King's Scholars, which is the origin of the King's School now educating rather more.

Here we see the Great Gate to St Augustine's Abbey and College, locally known as Fyndon's Gate, by Lady Wootton's Green, built under the instructions of Abbot Fyndon between 1301 and 1309. There's a hedge where that fence runs, bottom right, and a few new traffic signs, but the biggest difference is on the left side of the gate as we look. Bomb damage resulted in rather unsympathetic restoration in new stone, which is especially visible on that tower. Otherwise the great works stand as our picture shows, although you can't see the houses around that were flattened by the bombs.

Probably the best known view of all is that of the Norman Staircase (overleaf), which, as you might expect, hasn't changed at all.

Along with Canterbury Cathedral and the abbey, St Martin's Church now forms a UNESCO World Heritage Site. Saint Martin was a childhood convert, then a Roman soldier and the Bishop of Tours, who cured the sick, raised the dead to life, cast out devils, and is the patron of this very old church, which was probably Queen

Bertha's private chapel to start with, although Roman bricks and other clues indicate something even earlier.

Certainly it is the oldest parish church in England still in use. According to the traditional story, this was where King Æðelbryht was baptised, thus giving powerful royal approval to Augustine's mission and so it can be regarded as the mother church for the whole of the Anglican communion.

Our picture of the interior looks from the nave through the Early English period arch (early 1200s) to the chancel, which is the oldest part, the original church. The altar in Victorian times was decorated rather more ornately than it is today.

The churchyard holds the graves of some famous people, including the creator of Rupert Bear, Mary Tourtel, and some not so famous. Our picture opposite reminds us of the dreadful rate of child mortality before the age of modern medicine. Annie Emily, daughter of Thomas and Emily James, born May 27th 1855, died February 17th 1868. Alice Rhodes died November 18th 1864, aged five years and eleven months; Arthur Rhodes, died December 5th 1873 aged 27 days; Florence Rhodes, died April 20th 1874 aged nine years and seven months.

The stones are worn and weathered now. They somehow seem more poignant when new.

W.E. HARRISON.
HIGH CLASS PRINTER
MANUFACTURING STATIONER
THE ANCIENT HOUSE PRINTING PRESS

Chapter Eleven

The Day We Went to Ipswich

—⁂—

The Ancient House, parts of which were put up in the fifteenth century to house the family of one Sir Richard of Martlesham, later belonged to a wealthy fish merchant, then the Sparrowe family, who had it for 300 years. It used to be known as Sparrowe's house, and it must have been one of them who hid King Charles II after his final defeat at the battle of Worcester, if the King did hide at Sparrowe's, after he'd finished hiding in that tree and causing hundreds of pubs to be called the Royal Oak.

This view, from Dial Street, is much the same, except that the huge spectacles on the wall, low centre left, have gone, and the street light, and Messrs W.S. Harrison, High Class Printer and Manufacturing Stationer is no longer there. Mr Harrison bought his business from Frederick Pawsey in 1897, so that dates the picture to very shortly after. The Harrison family ran the business, there and in larger premises, until 1971, and it's now Ancient House Press plc on the Hadleigh Road Industrial Estate. In the shop today is a firm offering an unrivalled collection of creative kitchenware, practical ideas for the home and garden, and inspiring gifts from all over the world, it says here.

Ipswich is a Saxon name, *Gipeswic*, dwelling place on the river Gipping. Most people think of Ipswich as being on the Orwell, which is what the Gipping becomes as it widens out and heads for the sea, and there we have the reason for Ipswich: continental trade. Other industries in Victorian times were agricultural engineering, animal feed and fertiliser; they were the tractor boys.

Chapter Twelve

Somerset – Dunster and Minehead

—⁘—

The valleys are in general very rich; and many of the hills, a few years since undisturbed by the plough, are now well cultivated and produce large crops of grain. Hemp, flax, teazels and woad are cultivated in considerable quantities; the dairies produce some of the finest cheese in the Kingdom. The sheep indigenous to the county are the Mendip breed, but lately every other improved system has been introduced by its eminent and spirited cultivators. The cattle are nearly the same as those of Devon, and the teams of the opulent farmers may vie with those of any other county.

The climate of this county is various: near the sea-coast winter is scarcely felt; and from Minehead and Dulverton on the west, to Milborne Port and Wincanton on the east (excepting some of the eminences) it is mild and temperate.

So wrote a commentator of the Victorian period. The view is of Minehead, where winter was scarcely felt about 75 BB (Before Butlins). Woad in herbal medicine is a disinfectant and styptic, but mainly the woad plant was a source of blue dye for textiles, which fact goes nicely with the teazels. These would have been the fuller's teazel, whose dried heads were used to comb up the nap on 'the principle Manufactures of this county ... broad and narrow fine woollen cloths and a variety of coarse woollen goods.' The hemp and flax were made into 'coarse linens, comprising dowlases, tickings etc.' For those of us more used to shopping at Marks and Sparks, dowlas was a stout, strong cloth used when long and hard wear were the most important attributes.

Dunster has two reasons for being there: the cloth industry and its harbour, both well established by the thirteenth century. There was even a type of cloth called Dunsters and, when the King sent a circular to all his ports of the realm, the only recipients in Somerset were Bridgwater and Dunster.

There was always trouble with the haven silting up. It got worse in mid-millennium so when a port was made at Minehead in the fifteenth century, Dunster's was usurped. The lords of the manor, the Luttrells, saw what was coming and gave Minehead a stone harbour. Dunster haven gradually disappeared back to nature.

The Yarn Market, in the centre of our picture, was built around 1600 to provide a new facility for keeping the local economy going, and it worked apart from an awkward period during the Civil War, when the Luttrells changed sides from Parliament to King Charles. In the siege of 1645, the castle hardly took a scratch while the town was badly beaten about.

Business recovered but more trouble was looming. Up north, a revolution was under way, with automatic machines and clogs, and poor old Dunster was left behind. By the end of the 1700s the place was in a parlous state, so its worthies redirected business towards a more general kind of market town and things looked up again.

The good news is that lack of money at crucial times meant little modernisation, so here was a rare example of an ancient town, preserved, for visitors to see. The Taunton to Minehead Railway arrived in 1874 and suddenly there was a new industry: tourism.

Dunster high street dates from the late 1100s, and the plots of land fronting on to the street, granted by the lord of the manor for rent and called burgages, are much the same now as they were then. Of course the houses are very different and there were no shops in those days. There were market stalls filling the street, including some for selling fish and some set up for slaughter and sale of meat (shambles). Crosses were erected to signify points of sale for butter, corn and so on, and stocks were fixed for village miscreants.

From about 1600, the Yarn Market co-existed with the shambles and whatnot until all that old stuff was demolished c.1825, except for the fifteenth century Butter Cross, which was re-erected on the Ellicombe road. The famous octagonal market

hall has a central stone pier supporting a stout timber framework and eight gabled dormers with wood mullions. The wood lantern shows 'GL 1647', the year it was repaired after cannonball hits in the siege.

Mr Crocker's (centre right) bicycles are not in evidence, the General Warehouse (centre left) no longer dyes cloth and the pub just below it is no longer. The two strollers and the cart have been replaced by crowds of grockles, bus stops, traffic lights, cars parked everywhere and other accoutrements of modernity, and somebody has cleared up the horse dung (bottom left). The trees at the top have gone but not those houses, and the Luttrell Arms (former residence of the Abbots of Cleve) on the right-hand side still sticks out slightly.

Conygar Tower, top right, was the 1775 folly of Henry Luttrell, 2nd Earl of Carhampton. It's 60 feet high and is where it is so that the Earl could see it from the castle.

Milling in Dunster was the cause of a great many disputes and hell-neighbourly fractiousness, because so many millers and others wanted to take advantage of the lord of the manor's mill leat, which was cut from the river Avill west of Frackford and ran next to the road that became the A396 West Street, before turning down Mill Lane (naturally), round the castle foot and back into the river.

Our picture shows the manorial corn mill, called Castle Mill, but upstream of that were all sorts of fulling, dyeing and tucking mills, not there now, and various sneaky people who would rob the mill stream to irrigate their land. Tucking, by the way, was a finishing process for cloth after weaving, when it was stretched on tenter hooks.

Blockages of the leat occurred regularly and the pollution was appalling. Things got so bad that the Luttrell of 1492 prohibited the cloth men from discharging their effluent except after normal working hours. When one of the fullers decided to go into flour instead, Lord Luttrell wasn't having it. It was his leat, so he eliminated the competition by diverting the stream to miss that mill altogether.

Our mill is on the site of two much earlier ones. It was rebuilt around 1780 but was abandoned soon after, and the result is our picturesque Victorian semi-ruin. It was fixed up around 1940, closed in 1962 but restored again as a working mill with the two overshot wheels you can see. It's privately owned, looking rather smarter than it does here, and the ivy has been taken off the ornate entrance.

Of all positions of strength for a castle, Dunster has one of the very best. The sea used to come up to the western face of this steep-sided hill and, with fortifications on the other, the early local lords, who were Saxons of Wessex, made the place pretty well impregnable, although it ceded to the Normans without a fight. William the Conqueror gave it to William de Moyon/Mohun and made him Sheriff of Somerset, and his son – yet another William – became the 1st Earl of Somerset. From such conventional beginnings, the story gets tricky.

The Mohuns built a new stone castle, which was besieged sometime around 1145 by King Stephen, the family having declared for Stephen's wife and rival, the Empress Matilda. When Matilda's son Henry II acceded, starting the Plantagenet dynasty, the right-sided Mohuns were launched on a period of prosperity. The castle expanded, and by 1266 consisted of hall with buttery, pantry, kitchen, bakehouse, chapel, knights' hall, with three towers and a prison in the upper ward, plus three towers and a granary in the lower ward, plus more by the river – shippon, stables, dovecote and dairy.

Meanwhile, the fortunes of the de Luterel/Luttrell family were on the up too, with Sir Geoffrey of that ilk, favourite minister of King John, acquiring the nearby manor of East Quantoxhead. Around 1330, Sir John Luttrell married Joan de Mohun; their son, Andrew, married Elizabeth de Courtenay, one of nineteen children of the Earl of Devon (see also page 151, Exeter Canal). Andrew and Elizabeth were granted a royal stipend of £200 a year and, when he died, she had the £200 all to herself and looked for something to spend it on.

Sir John de Mohun, lord of the manor of Dunster, having no sons, conveyed the castle to trustees for the use of his wife after he died. When he did, in 1376, Elizabeth came in with ready money as an offer for the reversion, that is, the castle would come to her when Lady de Mohun died. Her scheme didn't work because she died first.

Her son, Sir Hugh Luttrell, one eighth a de Mohun, had inherited East Quantoxhead and decided he should have Dunster too. The dowager Lady de Mohun died in 1404, and it all got very messy. Sir Hugh moved in for Christmas 1405, and his claim, contested by the remaining de Mohuns, went through the courts. The case was adjourned in 1407 and never revived, so that was the Luttrells installed for 600 years – with a short intermission.

During the Wars of the Roses, Sir James Luttrell, a staunch Lancastrian supporter, was knighted at the Battle of Wakefield and killed at the Second Battle of St Albans, so when Yorkist Edward IV won the throne, he threw the Luttrells out of Dunster. They had to forfeit the estate and all rights (act of attainder) to a Yorkist commander, Sir William Herbert, a Welsh baron known as Black William, who became the 1st Earl of Pembroke. Alas for him, the war swayed the other way and he was executed after losing the Battle of Edgecote Moor.

Hugh Luttrell was reinstalled in 1485, when the Lancastrians were finally victorious at Bosworth Field, and there was no more trouble for a while. In any case, the family preferred their seat at East Quantoxhead.

Along came George Luttrell, another Sheriff of Somerset and apparently a well liked fellow, who moved back into the castle in the late 1500s and built a mansion house in the lower ward, which is still there, also Minehead harbour and Dunster yarn market.

He didn't live to see the Civil War start, when his son Thomas declared for Parliament. A Royalist army turned up in 1643 and Thomas switched sides. The forces of Parliament arrived in 1645, besieged the castle, the garrison surrendered in 1646 and Thomas, noting the position of the butter on his bread, declared for Cromwell again, which loyalty lasted for almost a year until he died in 1647.

The walls had been damaged during the siege, and an order to demolish the castle altogether was issued in 1650. Some dismantling was done, which is mainly why so little of the medieval castle remains, but the house was refurbished and that's the way things stayed. It belongs to the National Trust now.

Dunster Castle and town in the 1730s, from a Buck Brothers engraving.

Dunster Priory Church of St George has some Norman work, including the round-arched west doorway in the picture. Building was begun in 1090, or soon after, when the aforesaid William de Mohun, the first Norman in the castle, and his wife Adeliza, gave the Saxon church with certain lands and tithes to the Bishop of Bath. In return for his gift, William stated in the deeds that the monks of Bath Cathedral priory were to rebuild the church, to make it bigger and better.

This was all very well but Bath was a long way away, too far for matters to be properly managed from there, so a small group of monks, a cell, was set up locally. We know the priory had a garden and a vineyard, but records are otherwise thin until, as is often the case with historical research, we come across a legal dispute.

In 1282, the priors of Dunster and of Stogursey argued over who should have the tithes of the village of Shurton. Dunster won the case, and by 1291 the priory had an annual temporal income (from property) of £5 13s 3d, about £65,000 modern equivalent, and a spiritual income, from ecclesiastical dues, of £13 7s 4d, about £150,000 modern.

Some years after that, the priory became more or less independent of Bath although still tied to it. The prior of 1332, Robert de Sutton, was given an annual income of £20. The value of money had gone down somewhat since 1291 so the prior only had about £165,000 (modern) a year. He was also to have such companions as he might choose, sent from Bath, with the right of sending them back if he didn't like them.

The monks and the good folk of Dunster shared the church, and in 1357 the problems with this arrangement caused the prior to set down some rules by which both groups had to abide. This was all right for a hundred years and more, during which most of the church our visitors could see, and we can see now, was built in Perpendicular style.

Towards the end of the 1400s the dispute blew up again, and this time it could not be resolved. It went to arbitration, in Glastonbury, and for judgement the arbitrators turned to Solomon and cut the church in half. The result was the marvellous oak rood screen in the picture, which goes right across the building, and a new choir, so the church had (and has) two choirs, one thirteenth century, one fifteenth. The parishioners used the western half of the church and the monks the east.

Forty years later, Henry VIII dissolved the priory. The property ended up with the Luttrells, was sold, then much later bought back again. Under the George Luttrell of Victorian times, the church, now fairly dilapidated, was restored to the fine state of the photographs and, inside or outside, the church hasn't really changed since then. Sir Hugh Luttrell, Lady Elizabeth Luttrell and various other Luttrells lie still within, remembered in sculpture.

In the general exterior view the size of the building to the right, with the gable end and vertical slit, indicates its importance. It's the old tithe barn, now a major restoration project.

On the left (overleaf) is No. 3 Castle Hill, Dunster. On the other side of the road, with the half-timbered gable end, is No. 6. The rather strange little girl with the unsettling face sits on the step of what is now Nos. 2 and 4. They are seventeenth-century, these houses, three of the 200 and more listed buildings in Dunster.

Brook Cottage and Old Stream Cottage are in a highly picturesque group of thatched houses on Park Street (page 91), that leads down to the river and the old packhorse crossing called Gallox Bridge. These are seventeenth-century too, and listed, of course.

No motor car would have yet been along Park Street as we can see it, so it's not too hard to imagine the packhorses toiling up the hill with their loads of wool yarn,

spun by grandmothers, wives and daughters on distant farms, heading for the market and their hard-wrung rewards for a hard life.

Here, these cottages look a lot more as they did when built, two or three hundred years before the photographs, than they do today. Today, they're neat and tidy, with time and money spent on them by proud owners. Their owners in 1890 or so didn't have time or money, so the cottages were straggly and scruffy and entirely without facilities for television reception. There are still gates on Castle Hill; different gates, but wooden gates nevertheless. No. 6 is an art gallery. Nos. 2 and 4 have a new porch roof and no ivy. The cobbles at the front have been extended, so cars can park there. You can go and see them. Take this book with you and spot the differences.

Overleaf, looking towards Blue Anchor Point with its alabaster rocks, along what is now the B3191, we could hardly have a view more altered in modern times. There's a wide road with yellow lines, a concrete prom and sea wall with big railings, and caravans behind you. You can see the Blue Anchor Inn upper right with the three chimneys. That's still there, but all the other old buildings have gone. No more thatched farmhouse, stone walls and sheds; just a few modern villas on the landward side.

91

An earlier travel writer noted, after the West Somerset Railway put Blue Anchor on a loop in 1874, that:

> There is a pleasant little bay here which possesses possibilities as a future watering-place, but at present the accommodation for visitors is extremely limited. Blue Anchor, a small hamlet clustered around the station, is probably named after the Blue Anchor Inn, a long-established hostelry situated at the east end of the long causeway.

The railway tried to solve the accommodation problem in 1936 with camping coaches – old carriages converted to the railway equivalent of a mobile home or youth hostel. Now the matter is finally resolved with a million caravans.

Around Blue Anchor Point, these days part of an SSSI and especially interesting to geologists, fossils can be found, including fish, reptiles, early small mammals and coprolites, which are lumps of fossilised dung. You will be pleased to know that ostracods, a sort of miniature prehistoric cross between a shrimp and a clam, are also abundant there.

Present-day fish are much sought, by anglers leaning their rods on the prom railings.

> The bold, wooded North Hill gives Minehead a distinctive and pretty situation. Round the ancient, picturesque village has grown a modern, well built town climbing the hill slopes and stretching along the level ground beside the Bristol Channel.

Thus related a 1930s' guidebook, but the modern town had not been built when our visitors went. The old place was in three hamlets: on the hill, Higher Town; at

the foot, Middle Town; and Quay Town. They made their livings mostly out of herring and wool, and so declined when the fish left and the wool went north.

St Michael's church is on the upper left edge of our photo, but the hill is dominated by a Victorian excess, Elgin Towers, supposedly a replica of a Scottish castle, and it certainly looks like one. It was commissioned in 1887 by Kennedy Cooke, a Scot who made his pile out of sweeties then inflicted this pile on the fishermen of Minehead. Nowadays, it's largely hidden by trees.

Much of what you can see straggling along at the hill foot is Quay Street, still there as listed buildings. The one with the five gables, behind our couple sitting on the bench, is Coastguard Cottages, on the corner of Quay Street and Quay Lane.

The big differences between this and the modern view are the mass of houses where we have open fields, below and to the left of Elgin Towers, and the hill is more wooded now, altering its shape to the distant eye. We have just a little bit of Warren Road bottom left, where there is now a massive sea wall and promenade. Our couple sitting there, she listening so attentively, could not have anything like that peace and quiet today.

By the river Washford, between the villages of Hungerford and Washford, lie the remarkably well preserved remains of Cleeve Abbey, a monastery founded by a scion of the de Roumare family (earls of Lincoln) at the end of the twelfth century, and

staffed by Cistercian monks from the earlier abbey at Revesby, Lincolnshire, which in turn had been staffed by monks from the premier house of Rievaulx, Yorkshire.

Cleeve is especially notable because such substantial remnants, including the gatehouse (page 96) and refectory we see here, of which a king could be proud, come from an abbey that never amounted to much when it was functional. It never got above thirty monks, was often in financial straits and, with a poor lot of abbots through the 1300s, ran up large debts with London merchants. A reputation was gained for, shall we say, indiscipline.

Matters improved greatly in the fifteenth century, when most of the major building work was done, but the low income ensured that the abbey was chopped in the first round of Henry VIII dissolutions in 1536. Luckily, they only wrecked the church, leaving the rest more or less intact to become a very posh house for a short time, leased from the Earl of Sussex by one Anthony Busterd, after which the buildings served as a farmstead for 300 years.

In 1870, our friend George Luttrell stepped in, bought the place, kicked out the farm animals and began some archaeological and restoration work, so when our visitors went they could view in civilised manner. The abbey gatehouse looks a little cleaner and smarter now without the ivy, likewise the refectory, under the care of English Heritage.

Chapter Thirteen

The Day We Went to Bristol

*B*ristol Cathedral began as an abbey in 1140, populated by a religious order of Augustinian Canons, or Black Canons, for the colour of their cassocks. These were not the Augustinian Friars, who were monks, but rather clerics who ministered to the people while following the rules of life laid down by St Augustine of Hippo.

The abbey went through various phases of building and rebuilding, which was still going on when Henry VIII put a stop to it and reversed some of the work by having part of the church knocked down and the rest closed.

In 1542, Archbishop Thomas Cranmer's efforts to create a separate diocese in Bristol were officially confirmed by the King and the old church was split off from the diocese of Worcester, restyled as the Cathedral of the Holy and Undivided Trinity, and made the seat of the 1st Bishop of Bristol.

Nothing much happened after that until the Victorian wave of enthusiasm for Gothic architecture provided the impetus for a new nave, very like the one Henry had demolished, to be built and the western front, seen in our picture, was remodelled with twin towers. All this was finished only in 1888, just in time for our visitors, and we can surmise that the taxi rank came about to cater for all those wishing to see the latest improvements. The taxis have gone, of course, and the railings, and there's no bench for an old man to sit and smoke his pipe, at half past ten in the morning or any other time, ignoring the cathedral as he looks across College Green at the Council House.

The Society of Merchant Venturers, a group largely devoted to exploring the world and expanding trade therewith from Bristol, acquired the Manor of Clifton in 1676. Part of this rural estate was the 200+ acres known as the Clifton Down, on the edge of the Avon Gorge. When the Manor of Henbury came up for sale two centuries later, including a similar kind of area called Durdham Down, Bristol Corporation bought it on the understanding that Clifton and Durdham Downs would be managed by the Adventurers for the recreation of the citizens of that fair city.

By this time, Clifton had become an inland spa resort and traditional rural pursuits, such as cattle grazing, had ceased. Gentrification had become a threat. Wealthy folk were building grand residences and the people's park was in need of formal measures to preserve it, resulting in the Clifton and Durdham Downs Act 1861.

We can't tell if our couple by the park bench on page 100 knew each other well. Somehow, the lady's parasol and the angle of the gentleman's stick seem to suggest not. Perhaps, after a nice chat about the excellent facilities provided by the Downs Committee and a quiet rest on the bench, they will go their separate ways, or decide to meet again.

The view of the Clifton Suspension Bridge is very much the same today. The little kiosk has gone and the hillside trees are more numerous, but if you wanted a picture with nothing on the bridge except someone who seems to be pushing a handcart, you'd have to stage it or paint it.

Chapter Fourteen

Exmoor – Lynton and Lynmouth

The Ship Inn, Porlock (overleaf), on our holidaymakers' way to Exmoor, claims to have been established in the thirteenth century and that may be so. You will notice nowadays that the brick extension to the chimney stack has gone, likewise all the thatched roofs around except for the inn's. The house on the right beyond the inn has made way for a wider road, and Hawkins the Baker at the bottom of the hill, has been replaced by houses set back for modern traffic. A sketch to hand from 1928 shows our photo to be accurate at least until then.

We could not have asked for a better selection of men from Porlock than appear here. Our top-hatted gent with the fringe beard seems a little embarrassed by being asked to pose, motionless, arms by his sides, while the other two, whose feet the photographer has unfortunately cut off, stand in easy conversation, the old mariner type and the eager young bowlered bank clerk.

The porched inn doorway where they stand is no longer in use but the inn remains as popular and stately a pleasure dome as it ever was. Sam Coleridge, a poet who knew something about pleasure domes and old mariners, lived in nearby Nether Stowey and, according to the story, was composing *Kubla Khan* in The Ship when he was famously put off his stroke by 'a person on business from Porlock'.

Writers everywhere now complain about any interruption as being by 'a man from Porlock' or they merely say they've had 'a Porlock', but we can't believe the story. If Coleridge was in The Ship, in Porlock, why would he note the departure point of a man coming in off the street?

There are 120 square miles of Exmoor over 1,000 feet above sea level but our visitors have stayed in the more accessible, sheltered parts near the coast. The Royal Forest of Exmoor, that is, the 'king's hunting ground', was established in medieval times in the middle of the moor, roughly 20,000 acres (well over 8,000 hectares) of wild and inhospitable country, home to red deer and the native ponies. Sheep farming for wool rather than meat was the mainstay of the poor families who tried to scratch a living up there, spinning their harvest into thread on the farm to be taken by merchants to Dunster and other markets, where it was sold on for finishing into cloth.

Land enclosure began quite early in the medieval period and larger estates developed from the 1600s onwards. In 1818, a fellow who'd made his fortune bashing metal in Birmingham bought much of the Royal Forest. He was John Knight, and he and his son began a long battle with the climate, trying to institute lowland and arable advanced farming methods and, largely, failing. Soon after our visitors were here, in 1897 the Knight estate was bought by Earl Fortescue, who saw the sense in old fashioned grazing.

The view (page 103) is of the coastal edge of Exmoor, looking at Countisbury Hill from the village of Lynton, with Lynmouth out of sight beneath. The hill is more wooded now, so some of the buildings we can see in our picture are partly hidden away, but not the big one in the middle, the Tors Hotel. As we would expect, there has been more development in the river valley and by the shore, as the tourist industry has grown way beyond Victorian levels.

Well, my friends, what a change is here. Looking up Mars Hill in Lynmouth, the building on the right and partly behind us, being Knight's Sea Breeze Cottage Apartments with Cloak Room, is now Sea Breeze Cottage. It is also the Sea Breeze gift shop. Above that, where we have private houses or possibly more apartments, today is the Rising Sun Hotel, looking like it's always been there although we can see no signs in our picture. The hotel's PR says it is partly comprised of fourteenth-century fishermen's cottages, which would be staggering if true, frequented by smugglers, of course. It also hosted R.D. Blackmore while he was writing *Lorna Doone*, and had P.B. Shelley as guest for his honeymoon with his girl bride Harriet Westbrook. That would be in Shelley's Cottage, No. 1 Mars Hill, which is

seventeenth or eighteenth-century, still mostly thatched and around the corner behind the big house, late eighteenth-century, at the top of the hill, also now part of the Rising Sun, as is the rest of the row (seventeenth and eighteenth-century).

The poetic connection is also claimed by Shelley's Hotel, although the eloping couple, he nineteen, she sixteen, seem to have lodged with a Mrs Hooper at Woodbine Cottage, which isn't an address anymore but could now be part of an hotel. Later, one winter's night, in despair at Percy's extramarital doings, Harriet walked into the Serpentine and drowned herself, and her ghost still searches the guest houses of Lynmouth trying to find the right one.

While there can be no doubt about any of that, we can see down the road to the left, which is Lynmouth Street, a prominent white house. It still stands but it's a shop, and the harbour wall, rebuilt after the flood of 1952 (see below) has been moved to our left to make a wider road.

On any holiday here now, instead of our very small population in the photo, there are hundreds of folk thronging the streets, and a line of cars parked on the left. Our four models are alone. The two younger ones seem to have moved during the exposure, while the older girl and the fellow on the left have maintained their poses.

Looking down Mars Hill, the tiled, many-sided turret is still there, with another gift shop beneath. The harbour's more or less the same as when built in the eighteenth century, except much tidier and with small cruisers and speed boats in

it. All the stone surfaces are now straight and neat, nothing is ramshackle, the tower looks more businesslike – and there's a reason for that. The Rhenish Tower you see in our picture was washed away in the flood and the harbour walls and quay were much damaged. The Tower, called Rhenish for its architectural style, was rebuilt from picture-postcard references, its originator, a General Rawdon, who had it as a saltwater reservoir for his bath, having neglected to leave the plans.

Otherwise, we nowadays see sturdy railings, there's no fishing gear lying about, and there are trippers on the benches rather than the old boys of Lynmouth. Here we see them chuntering on about how things aren't as good as they were when the bonny shoals provided an honest living (supplemented by the smuggling) and before they made guesthouses out of the kipper sheds.

The herring apparently left suddenly, in seventeen something, vexed from overfishing by men forced to it, the parson demanding ever rising tithes in fish.

The East Lyn River starts way up on Exmoor, flows past Brendon and joins Hoar Oak Water at Watersmeet (see page 114). Gentle woodland becomes narrow gorge for the larger stream, then flattens out where sister river West Lyn, similarly sourced, comes in at Lynmouth. Our visitors, looking at this sweet especial rural scene, with its brown trout in crystal waters and wagtails bobbing on the rocks, might also have had a look at the nation's first hydro-electric power station completed in 1890, and doubtless would have been told that Lynmouth was the second town in the country to be supplied with the new miracle, electricity.

However, they cannot have imagined this same river in such a fury that thirty-four people would die. Sixty or so years later, on the night of 15 August 1952, after more than 9 inches (230 mm) of rain had fallen within twenty-four hours up on the Exmoor tops, disaster struck. The ground there was already sodden and could not absorb such a huge quantity, so the water found its own way down. Streams became torrents, trickles became roaring waterfalls, and still there was nothing like enough capacity to cope. Rivers were formed on the instant, creating new courses by sheer force, and pouring into the East and West Lyns, which were already swollen beyond all bounds.

Trees were pulled from their roots. Telegraph poles, cars, anything in the water's path including the famous power station, was picked up and hurled downstream, to smash against bridges, blocking the raging waters until they too had to give way. Thousands of tons of rocks filled the streets and, as the flood receded, many more thousands of tons of debris were exposed, from the hillsides and the sixty buildings that were thrown down.

A mile or two to the west is a violent scene in the sharp and jagged granite outcrops and pinnacles of the Valley of Rocks, a short coombe with no river in it. Naturally, the more notable of the peaks have acquired names. Here we see Ragged Jack, the dominating Castle Rock with its sheer drop to the sea, and the Cheesewring. Beyond Castle Rock is Duty Point.

Not to be confused with the Cheesewring on Bodmin Moor, Cornwall, this is the Devil's Cheesewring, haunt of wild goats, which don't appear to be doing much of a job of clearing the Cheesewring from its vegetation, and don't appear elsewhere on Exmoor either.

There are strong associations between this landscape and *Lorna Doone*, not the author R.D. Blackmore's favourite work but easily his most successful. In 1865, he and wife Lucy came on holiday here, where he heard about Aggie Norman of Lynton, recently dead at the age of 83. He may even have known her when he came here to his grandfather's on his school vacations. Aggie was supposed to be a witch and she used to live in the Valley of Rocks in the summer, by the Cheesewring, where people came to consult her about romantic and other matters. Thus was formed the character of Mother Meldrum in the novel.

Several Exmoor inns claim that the Blackmores lodged there while writing the book, including the Royal Oak at Withypool, the Rising Sun at Lynmouth and the Ship at Porlock.

A cheesewring, incidentally, for readers too young to remember what wringers were used for, especially on Mondays, was a kind of manually operated press to squeeze excess whey from cheese curds.

Lee Abbey, spelled Ley in our visitors' time, is the building to the right of the picture. We're looking down to Lee Bay. There is another Lee Bay, further along the coast beyond Ilfracombe, famous as a smuggler's cove (see page 136). As all able-bodied Devonians over the age of twelve were smugglers, doubtless this bay was similarly employed by the otherwise good folk of Lynton.

Duty Point is out of sight to the right, wherefrom Jennefried, the heiress to Ley Abbey, portrayed as Frida in R.D. Blackmore's story of that name, leaped to her

death. On her wedding day she discovered that the expected groom had married another, so she wandered off in the night, dressed in her wedding gown, to the cliff edge, and fell onto the unforgiving rocks below. The place is still known as Jenny's Leap.

We can see Crock Point below, and on to Woody Bay and Wringapeak. Much of this land was bought in 1628 by Hugh de Wichehalse, who turned the farmhouse at Ley into a more substantial residence. The Wichehalses left after a hundred years or so, and something like 9 acres of the land fell in the sea. The remainder was bought in 1841 by Charles Bailey, who built a new manor house a short distance away from the old farm. In the fashion of the time, he had it designed in the Gothic Revival style to resemble an ancient abbey. It later became an hotel, then a school, still called Lee Abbey although there had not been any religious connections since Norman times when the farm was owned by Forde Abbey in Somerset.

Now there are such connections, because Lee Abbey is a Christian community and retreat, home to the Lee Abbey Movement.

Watersmeet (overleaf), where the East Lyn River joins with Hoar Oak Water, has been a famous beauty spot since there were visitors to go and look at it. Described by a Victorian writer:

> The Lyn, which rises in the forest of Exmoor, is a small but rapid river, pursuing its impetuous course over rocks of immense size, and at length rushes into the British Channel.

It's National Park country now, of course, and the footpath you can see in the lower picture is the last leg of the Samaritans Way, which runs from Clifton Suspension Bridge to Lynton. The early Victorian fishing lodge, off to the left of our picture, is a National Trust café and tourist trap, so if you want to experience the mystery of this place, go before it opens at 10.30.

The East Lyn is itself formed of two streams that meet near the hamlet of Malmsmead, Badgworthy Water and Oare Water, and if you go further up you'll find Weir Water and Chalk Water meeting at Oareford, and tributaries into the high hills at 1,300 feet and more.

As our Victorian writer says, these streams are small but impetuous, and they have cut steep, narrow gorges and so must rush rather than meander. You may be lucky and see a salmon desperately obeying its undeniable urge to negotiate this

difficult route, leaping and tumbling from pool to pool in the rapids. Above you tower the gorge sides, covered in beech, oak and larch, undergrown with ferns and masses of flowers in season. It really doesn't take much imagination to see the Green Man somewhere in the trees ... in fact, that might be him there, just to the right of centre.

In Barbrook, the road you can see as it goes past St Bartholomew's church is the A39, bearing off to the left as the B3234 to Lynton. There's a socking great filling station where that little shed is, opposite the church, and instead of the minor road going over the old stone bridge and on up the hill, they've built a new bridge across the West Lyn gorge for the main road to Lynmouth and Porlock, more or less through the middle of those houses on the right.

There is more building, as you might expect, but not that much more. There's a village hall beyond the chapel and some houses beyond that where we just have allotments, and there's a bus shelter and a red phone box, but if you close your right eye and ignore the A39 ...

This magnificent sawmill, just yards downstream of the old Lyn bridge on the West Lyn River, was swept away in the flood of 1952. No trace of it remains, although the mill cottages survived.

Hunters' Inn, in the steep, wooded valley of the river Heddon, presents a very similar view today – at least, the valley does. The inn burned down in 1895, so the one you see today is in the same place but without the thatch. It has gables and overall is fairly similar to the original, which apparently began as a farmhouse or cottage, but with timbers showing in the Edwardian mock-Tudor style.

You can also expect to find a rather different set of vehicles in the car park, not that our vehicles in the picture had necessarily been used to get to the pub. The road you can see to the right, leading eventually by perilous dips and climbs to Lynton, was a favoured scenic carriage drive. There's the site of a small Roman fort at the top of the hill, doubtless not a favourite posting in the middle of nowhere with nothing to do but watch the sea.

Into that sea runs the river Heddon, joined by its several tributaries just by the inn. Here we show it at Heddon's Mouth, a picturesque spot that has changed hardly at all apart from a safer looking bridge, and still only accessible on foot or by boat. There is a designated picnic area, for those who need such designations, and the old lime kiln, which is that block-house object centre left, has been restored.

The walk down through the cleave (Devonian for gorge) is only a mile from the inn. Quite a lot of people do it now; very few would have done it in our visitors' day, but there would have been more fritillaries. Perhaps scholarly Victorians would have recognised the small pearl-bordered ones, and told them from the silver-washed.

Woody Bay, west of Lynton and Lynmouth, known as Wooda Bay in our visitors' time and at least until the 1930s, remains a good example of nature's obduracy in the face of human vanity and ambition. A wealthy lawyer called Colonel Lake bought it and the rest of the manor of Martinhoe in 1885, with the intention of turning the whole area into a genteel holiday resort. Various schemes such as a pier – built, destroyed soon after in a storm – and a railway – still partly there in the Lynton and Barnstaple narrow gauge line – were begun to try and bring in more visitors, but they cost him dearly and he ended up in debt and in clink.

Like so many of the valleys and bays on this part of the coast, Wooda Bay is inaccessible to large numbers of motor cars and therefore stays as it almost always was. There are a few hotels and villas, as you can see in the picture, but that's it and all about it.

A precipitous path makes its way down to a small rocky beach, an idyllic place where the only disadvantage, as one visitor put it, is the thought of having to climb back up again. There's another lime kiln and a cottage the lime burner used to live in, and you can see a few bits of the pier. The stream called Hanging Water hurries through the woods to a waterfall.

Although the bay is very woody indeed, it is unlikely that the name comes from that feature. If so, there should be another twenty woody bays at least. Possibly it's derived from the Saxon name of an early settler, or it could be from the Anglo-Saxon *wòd* and *wòda*, words meaning danger or madness, sometimes with implications of possession by the devil. Well, there are ghost stories around Wooda Bay ... .

A mile or so easterly upstream of Watersmeet on the East Lyn, and only a mile south from the coast's clifftops, is the little hamlet of Rockford. It was and is a few houses in a clearing, with a pub. Marvellous. Looking from this point of view today, out of sight there are a couple of private garages but otherwise there are no more buildings than there were in Victorian times.

In fact, there's one fewer. The old barn beside the pub has gone to make way for a modest car park. The hedge in front of the pub has been replaced by umbrellas and tables but the bridge looks the same, although it's a rebuild, our bridge having disappeared in 1952. It now connects to the Samaritans' Way and remains a favourite gazing place.

The Rockford Inn looks from the outside much the same as it did. Parts of the building are 1700s, which you can easily see in the lower bar, but it surely could not have been trading as an inn since then. Inns relied on passing trade and there can have been very little of that. Rockford is on the way to nowhere except Lynmouth, which wasn't big enough to be shown on Victorian maps. Only when the hunting, shooting, fishing and Exmoor holiday trades raised a demand can there have been enough business to support such a fine inn, or 'pub with rooms', as the modern phrase has it.

The fishing is still good. The river East Lyn is spawning ground for salmon fighting their way up the torrents from the sea, and there are resident brown trout, which may well be the subject of the discussion between our two elderly gents in the detail.

Chapter Fifteen

The Day We Went to Hythe

—ɯ—

The basic idea behind the Royal Military Canal, initially known as Mr Pitt's Ditch, after its proponent prime minister, was to defend against a Napoleonic invasion. It would run more or less from Hythe to Rye, turning Romney Marsh into a sort of island. It all looks a bit potty now and, when the canal was completed after many setbacks and huge expense, the threat of invasion was long gone and the canal had little use. The town of Hythe bought its stretch in the 1860s for leisure and pleasure, and there have been boats for hire at Ladies Walk Bridge ever since, as we see here.

Hythe no longer has a harbour, but it does have a seafront, and Ladies Walk was a nineteenth-century idea of a pathway with trees and formal gardens to permit a mile's gentle stroll between town and sea. Many byelaws were made in 1874 to govern its use. For example, a person shall not bring or cause to be brought into the pleasure ground any cattle, sheep, goats, or pigs, or any beast of draught or burden, unless in pursuance of an agreement with the Council, and a person shall not bring or cause to be brought into the pleasure ground any barrow, truck, machine or vehicle, unless used for the conveyance of a child or an invalid.

Everything looks much tidier now, especially on the far bank, and it's a different and sturdier bridge. In our picture we have our obvious poser in the boatman, standing slightly awkwardly by his business, but possibly of more interest is the stoutish chap having what looks like a stern word about a piece of mischief with the guilty boy on the bench. Well, what can we expect from the youth of yesterday?

Chapter Sixteen

Devon – Ilfracombe and Clovelly

—⫘—

The old coast road between Combe Martin and Ilfracombe has been partly superseded by the shortcuts of the A399, but here we are on that old road, looking across Combe Martin Bay to the Hangman headlands, Little and Great. We must be just past the Sandy Cove Hotel, or just before, really, as our holidaymakers are going in the other direction, towards Watermouth from Combe Martin, with a detour to Berrynarbor.

The same view now would show you caravans on Little Hangman, and around the corner another massive caravan and camping site, but we can shut our eyes to that and enjoy the view as it used to be. Our photographer has obviously got the driver to stop his horse in the middle of the road, long enough for the exposure. It looks a classy outfit, with a smart cabbie in bowler hat and some sort of decorations on the horse's head too.

The view of Combe Martin, featuring the church of St Peter ad Vincula (St Peter in chains), hasn't changed much. The hillside is possibly a little more wooded and the big tree on the left has gone but, remarkably, that's about it. The village, and romantic old fools like us, can thus be grateful for its situation, one long street in a narrow valley leading down to the sea, making the usual sorts of expansion difficult. There may not be so many fishing boats in the harbour, but the essence of the place is still there.

Combe Martin was a little fishing village like many others but struck it rich in minerals, in particular, silver, and men were imported from more traditional mining regions to work the seams. All gone now but a study of local genes might be

125

interesting. In later years it was famous for strawberries, and a travel writer of the 1920s described it as 'the Worthing of the west', whatever that may have meant at the time.

Berrynarbor, a village to the west of Combe Martin, was described thus in Victorian times:

> A parish and pleasant village, surrounded by beautiful woodland scenery, on an eminence near the sea-coast, overlooking Watermouth Cove, three miles east of Ilfracombe Railway Station. It is in Barnstaple union and county court district, Braunton petty sessional division, Ilfracombe polling district of North Devon, Braunton hundred, Barnstaple archdeaconry, and Sherwell rural deanery. It had 751 inhabitants (392 males, 359 females) in 1871, living in 159 houses, on 4,958 acres of land, including a range of hills in which lime and other stone are obtained.

By the census of 2001, the population had dropped by two to 749, not counting the transient denizens of the Mill Park campsite who have replaced the lime and other stone as a source of village income. Of course, there are some new houses, compared with our picture, but with Berrynarbor being an entirely impractical commute to anywhere sizeable, loss of agricultural workers has been made good by the usual mixture now found in villages and a kind of status quo preserved.

What you can see in this picture of Watermouth Bay has hardly changed. The lane is the A399, and the buoy's gone. The little tower up there on The Warren (detail overleaf), an eighteenth-century folly-cum-dovecot, is still standing, but what you can't see has changed enormously. The tranquil surface is covered with pleasure craft, hundreds of them, well, dozens anyway, floating or stranded depending on the tide, and on the right of the picture, where we have just a patch of bare ground, there are various small buildings to do with the holiday trade.

To our left, out of our sight, is Watermouth Castle Family Theme Park, and further up is a heated swimming pool, zip wire, bar, takeaway restaurant and launderette, not to mention 12 acres of lodges. Behind us to our right is a site

licensed for ninety caravans, with 'two fantastic caves for the whole family to enjoy!' and a private beach with 'Water! Hermit Crabs! Big Crabs and Small Crabs and plenty of other exciting sea life!!!'

Behind that again is 'a modern camping and caravanning park with all the facilities you would expect to find', including toilets, BBQ supplies, large dog exercise area and children's tractor rides (weather permitting).

When our visitors were travelling by, the only facilities they looked for were a bed for the night and sustenance along the way. If they had a large dog, specified exercise areas were not necessary, and the tractor had not yet been invented. Of course, their holidays were for the few, the privileged classes only. They had no impact on the environs. Large numbers of people didn't have holidays, so the countryside had no price to pay.

Our three main pictures of Ilfracombe show a general view taken from the top of the mount called Hillsborough, the harbour (page 130) with Hillsborough in the background, and (page 131) a look from around the corner to the west, with Hillsborough but also (page 132) the curious chapel of St Nicholas on Lantern Hill,

a fourteenth-century building with added lantern, said to be the oldest working lighthouse in Britain. You can also see this in the general view above, right centre.

The church in the foreground is that of St Philip and St James. The much older, partly Norman parish church hasn't much of a tower and so is hardly visible among the tumble of buildings beyond the high street. Among its many interesting features are stone corbels carved to represent Chichevache and Bycorn, the mythical bovines. The former was terribly undernourished as she only ate good women, while Bycorn grew fat on the more plentiful fodder of honest and long-suffering

husbands. This story seems to be too politically incorrect to feature in modern publicity.

The wooden jetty to the right has gone and there are cars parked where the carriages are in our picture. Below the tall building in the centre there are now the twin beehives, or are they power station cooling towers, of the Landmark Theatre. The old lifeboat station at the bottom of Lantern Hill is still there but is now an aquarium, and most of the seafront is recognisable by today's tourists, of which there are many.

Ilfracombe is the perfect location for North Devon holidays, offering you a gateway to an exciting blend of stunning coastal scenery, seaside fun, rural tranquillity and centuries of heritage and style. A stunning coastal town with whitewashed houses, grand Victorian villas and terraces, the 'jewel' of the North Devon coast is a remarkable location for romantic getaways, family holidays or activity breaks.

We can be sure our holidaymakers were unfamiliar with the idea of activity breaks, much less romantic getaways, but they would certainly have appreciated the rest.

Ilfracombe was more than a fishing port. International trade featured Wales, West Africa and the West Indies, and there were ferries, highly popular until the railway came. There are ferries still, only to Lundy Island, and no railway any more.

The Bethel mission is now Ilfracombe Yacht Club, and Mr Rowland's hotel is a smart café. In fact, it's very smart:

> The Quay Restaurant and White Hart Bar is the latest culinary expedition by Damien Hirst and is home to a unique and substantial collection of the artist's works with the Harbourside room dedicated to the Pharmacy theme and many other examples throughout using butterflies, fish and shells. Formerly The White Hart Inn, the classical fronted building has been beautifully restored and now

relates well to the stunning views out to the Atlantic and the traditional harbour of this ancient port.

Most of the rest of the buildings on the harbour front now house chippies, ice cream bars, gift shops and fudge shops, with a pub at either end. In our detail (page 130) we can see the good ship BE3, registered at Barnstaple under the Sea Fisheries Act of 1868. The two gentlemen stand outside what is now an art gallery.

As you can see, Ilfracombe is enclosed by hills and cliffs and getting to the beach was originally very difficult, depending on the tide. After the railway came in 1874, with more and more people wanting to bathe, it was worthwhile to dig tunnels through the cliffs, one for each sex. Any cheeky chappie trying to get a butcher's at the ladies' beach, unless he was very careful crawling among the rocks, would be spotted by a watchful bugler and given a blast.

The heights of the Torrs, just west of Ilfracombe, used to be rather inaccessible until the zigzag footpath was made, which was a new tourist attraction when this photograph was taken. It was more of a bridleway, really, as it was used by horse-drawn traffic; our visitors would have been charged a penny toll to walk it. Also new at this time was that building below the Torrs to the left, and in the detail: the Granville Hotel, today an apartment block on the end of the fully built-up residential Granville Street.

From the Torrs it's only a couple of miles along the South West Coast Path to the village of Lee, wherein the modern person will have no trouble finding the Old Post Office, now a private house rather than one of Tea & Refreshment, offering Milk, Cream and Junkets, Fruits in Season (strawberries today, it says on the awning), and Carriages for Hire.

This is not the disaster one might imagine, for the low buildings opposite, on the left of our picture, now form the Grampus Inn, where they will probably have everything except Junkets and Carriages.

Old Maid's Cottage looks a little different with the ivy all gone and the cliff face now overgrown instead. Its age is uncertain, probably mid 1600s, extended in Victorian times, possibly by the old maid in question. Our poser looks like he might be connected with the post office, which is 50 yards or so behind him. Perhaps that's his dad in the trap, holding his horse so steady and neat.

Lee Bay is popular with surfers now; of old, those riding the waves to shore were more used to carrying contraband. Yes, it's smugglers again, only here we have hard evidence. On 23 June 1786, sixty-six bottles of gin, thirteen gallons red Portugal wine, 250lb white salt and seventy-three packs of playing cards without the ace of spades, were seized from John Beer at Lee. The ace of spades was the duty card, signifying tax had been paid; at this time, all aces of spades were officially printed by a government department, which included the royal coat of arms in the design.

In 1820, a certain Mr Cook of Ilfracombe was reported to have landed 300 five-gallon casks of gin and brandy at Lee, which were 'carried into the interior'. You bet they were, and we have no reason to suppose that these were isolated incidents.

Our view of the bay (top) has most of the building and sea wall stonework behind us. That house no longer stands alone – there's another behind – and there are more trees around, and the road up to Woolacombe is much reinforced on the left of our picture. The shed in the centre has gone but that stream running across the rocks where our man bends to pick mussels – you can still see that at low tide.

Woolacombe Bay seen from the heath land beside Challacombe Hill presents the same view geographically but mankind has filled in the gaps between the buildings with more hotels and guesthouses. Woolacombe has no bathing machines on its miles and miles of golden sand but visitors come from half a dozen campsites, which illustrates the point. If there is room for large numbers of folk in a given place, they will be accommodated. In the 1920s, Woolacombe was described by the eminent author S.P.B. Mais:

> Woolacombe is an entirely new and comfortable holiday place ... wide sands hard enough for cricket and tennis ... will never be crowded, however thickly they cram Boy Scouts' and Girl Guides' camps along its fringe.

Our Boer War style tents on Barricane shell beach are not for Scouts or Guides. It's too early for that anyway, but they are the Victorian equivalent of the Portakabin-style café that now stands just behind the nearest tent.

The old bridge across the river Torridge at Bideford still carries traffic for the A386 but beyond it now are the soaring arches of the new bridge of the A39, crossing on the bend where that long spit of land comes out from the right.

In our picture we can see warehouses. That big one on the far side of the bridge, right-hand side, has gone but the nearside one with the rows of four windows is still there, smartened up into apartments. Otherwise it's mainly a question of more, on the hills to the right, not so much beyond on that side, but much filled in on our left towards the new bridge.

The Long (old) Bridge is thought to be thirteenth-century and has twenty-four arches of different widths. Nobody knows why. Two of them fell in 1968, so the new bridge had to be built.

Bideford has many famous sons and daughters, some of them called Grenville, but a particularly interesting one is Sir William Coffin. He was an important figure at the court of Henry VIII; so important that he could get away with attempted murder and GBH.

Passing by the churchyard one day, he noted a kerfuffle and inquired the cause. It seemed that the parson was refusing to perform a funeral service unless he had the dead man's family's only cow as payment (called a mortuary, a traditional if not entirely discretionary gift to the funeral officiator). Sir William had the meddlesome priest put in the grave – an exceptionally bold thing to do in those days – and the good citizens set about burying him alive until, almost interred, he relented. Sir William made so much of his story that a law was passed, thenceforth regulating the payment of mortuaries.

Clovelly? There's a lot less ivy and the wires of modernity are draped here and there, but little else has changed. It's tidier and neater, but in our visitors' day it was more a working place, not a time warp, although the task of preservation and pickling had begun.

It had been a fishing village until fame came, mainly through the activities of two people. The first was the author Charles Kingsley, a child of the village where father was rector, and he came back to write *The Water Babies* and *Westward Ho!*, the success of which had the same sort of effect that *Last of the Summer Wine* had on Howarth, or *The French Lieutenant's Woman* on Lyme Regis.

Responding to the tourists' call was Mrs Christine Hamlyn, wife of the village patriarch and owning family, who decided that Clovelly would be renovated to current – that is mid-nineteenth-century – standards, and kept that way. The impact of cars and trippers seen elsewhere has not happened in Clovelly and cannot happen. The Clovelly Estate Company owns all of the buildings and the land around, and Christine's legacy is not disturbed. You can't get a Range Rover in there anyway.

In our aerial view of the harbour, taken from Hobby Drive, the big building you can see on the pier is the Red Lion Hotel, partly eighteenth century on a much older site.

Hobby Drive was the private way from the big house to the village. To quote S.P.B. Mais again, 'It is, perhaps, the best way of approaching England's loveliest village. It winds gently downwards for three miles, affording glimpses through the rhododendrons and giant ferns of the quiet bay below.'

At the time our visitors were here, Clovelly had a population of about 600, declined somewhat from earlier years that had busier fishing. There's another thousand there now, catering for the tourists, as indeed is the famous hostelry, the New Inn. Or, should we say, the new New Inn, because the one our visitors saw, the one in the photograph, is not the one you see today. The old place was completely rebuilt.

Although often described as sixteenth or seventeenth-century, it is so only in style, although not far from the original. The official listing notes the date stone 'C.H. 1914', which stands for Christine Hamlyn, on whose orders the architects Burnett and Orphoot of Edinburgh designed it in 'Deliberately irregular plan, loose Tudor style' but seen through the eyes of William Morris and the Arts and Crafts movement.

The old sign we can see, with soldier and sailor on top for some reason swinging cricket bats around, was transferred to the new New Inn but it has gone, and there's a plainer one on the other side of the street, which is where the New Inn is.

In the harbour now are pleasure craft and fishing boats: 'George Cary of this place Esquire, in the last Age at his own charges built a pile or pier to resist the inrushing of the sea'. So that's the pier you can see on the left; Squire Cary lived 1543 to 1601, his family preceding the Hamlyns as lords of the manor.

The building on the right is Crazy Kate's Cottage, actually a pair of

cottages, which looks exactly the same today apart from a couple of roof lights and the railings painted white. Often said to be the oldest in the village, the cottages are probably eighteenth-century, so Crazy Kate Lyall and Mr Lyall may well have been the first occupants of new houses built on an old site because she died in 1736.

Her habit was to watch her husband out fishing in the bay, although where she got time to do that we don't know. Anyway, a squall turned his boat over and he drowned. She went mad with grief and one day put on her wedding dress, jumped off the pier and also drowned.

> To analyse its peculiar loveliness is not easy. Perhaps the fact that one walks out of the doorstep of one house on to the roof of the one below has something to do with it.

Certainly, Mr Mais, it surely has, and walking down the high street to the harbour one can go right under a house, which is Temple Bar Cottage in our picture, where the rooms over the arch made a shelter from the rain much beloved by the donkeys and their drivers.

The old lime kiln by the harbour – that roundish tower by the pointed archway – was fed by shipload of limestone and coal. In a region without its own limestone in the ground, but with lime needed by the farmers to spread on the land, most of the places where you could get a ketch to shore had a lime kiln. Clovelly's looks a little more symmetrical now than it does in our picture, having had its edges straightened.

Donkeys were the prime mode of transport upalong, with sledges being deployed on the rather easier downalong journeys, for goods, luggage and rubbish, and sometimes persons on the donkeys. Manpower does all the work now, apart from the carriage of juveniles for pleasure purposes.

So, goodbye Clovelly. Unique is a much overused term these days, often left to mean no more than unusual, but Clovelly was, and remains, unique in the true sense of the word. The old codgers may have gone but the rest, thanks to Mrs Hamlyn, is still there.

Chapter Seventeen

The Day We Went to Scarborough

—⚞—

There were old codgers in Scarborough too, posing so unselfconsciously. To quote a contemporary source:

> Though the Harbour and its vicinity suggest the lowlier haunts and occupations of men, and are quite distinct in charm and style from that to be found in the precincts of the fashionable South Cliff, with its select Esplanade and its choice gardens, yet it is to the lowlier quarter that most artists repair.

By 'artists' we clearly include photographers, always inclined to seek the lowlier haunts.

Spa waters were discovered in 1620 but little was made of that until bathing in the sea became popular in the 1700s, when Scarborough was able to market itself as doubly healthy and be described as the Queen of Watering Places and the first ever seaside resort.

Health was more fragile in earlier times. Harold Hardrada sacked and burned the place in 1066, to such effect that it got no mention in the *Domesday Book*. The Normans built a fine castle, which was all that was left standing when the Scots came in 1318, in one of their raids following victory at Bannockburn four years before. During the Civil

War, town and castle changed hands several times, eventually resulting in large parts of the castle being blown up.

Scarborough Fair began with a royal charter in 1253 and developed into a massive event lasting several weeks, with traders coming from mainland Europe and even further away, but you can't go to it now. You can go to the Spa, the large building in the centre of the picture of South Bay, opened in 1880, replacing the Joseph Paxton one that burned down in 1876, and signifying the increasing importance of music and entertainment over the doubtful qualities of the waters. There's rather more of the Spa now than in our visitor's time, with an open-air concert hall and some decidedly ugly modern carbuncles replacing that rather odd tower.

The South Cliff Tramway is still there, the first funicular railway in England, operated electrically these days, rather than by a combination of steam, water and gravity. So is the Grand Hotel up there centre right, unlike its glorious Victorian brethren, the Pavilion and the Balmoral, demolished to make way for vulgarity.

Chapter Eighteen

Exeter

—◁◁◁—

A contemporary of our visitors, travel writer Arthur H. Norway, said, 'In Exeter, all the history of the west is bound up.' At the time, and right up to the Second World War, all that history was there to be seen by everyone. German bombing changed the view and not always was the temptation resisted to replace the historic and beautiful with the ugly and cheap.

Our picture (previous page) shows the nature of the material with which the great cathedral is built – Beer stone, an easily workable limestone from the fishing village of Beer a few miles east of Exeter. It is white and soft initially but turns black, hard and crumbly with age. Further crumblings have been suffered by the carved saints on this, the west front, because of a superstition that stone powder rubbed from these holy statues could cure disease. That would have been mixed with powdered paint at first, because the whole of this vast face was brightly decorated.

In late Saxon and Norman times, Exeter was one of the richest cities in the country, thriving on the wool trade. In 1050, Leofric, Bishop of Crediton, moved his cathedra to Exeter, and in 1114, Bishop Warelwast, nephew of the Conqueror, started a new and huge cathedral church. It suffered through fires and various sieges but the two towers remain to represent Norman architecture, while the rest is largely in the Decorated style.

Bishop Grandisson built the west front, finished in 1342. By way of thanks, the Black Death visited Exeter in 1348 and reduced the population considerably, although leaving the good bishop untouched, possibly to write the great poem *Piers Plowman*. The other blackness, of the stone, has been removed for modern viewers.

Drake, Raleigh and Hawkins are supposed to have met to celebrate their seafaring deeds and plan further adventures in a room of a coffee house run by an Italian called Mol. The room, the one with the wonky windows on the first floor, seems very like a state cabin of a Tudor galleon, but the story, confidently quoted and widely believed, was concocted by an imaginative art dealer at the time our visitors were here, the man whose name is over the door in our picture, Thomas Worth.

In fact, the building and the house next door, here under the name of John Trickey, bootmaker, were put up by the bishop as quarters for priests. After the Reformation, the priests were kicked out and the buildings let for other purposes; our Mol's became a customs house, which was when the royal coat of arms was affixed in 1596. After 1661 it was an apothecary's shop, and a coffee house in or before 1726, when it was the business of a Mary Wilder, known as Molly. Other lady proprietors succeeded, keeping the name, and it remained a fashionable place of resort for eminent gentlemen until the 1830s, when it was translated into an artist's studio and gallery by a Mr John Glendall, painter and carver. He it was, probably, who painted the forty-six Devonshire family coats of arms in the famous room.

Thomas Burnett Worth turned the house into Worth & Co in 1878, whence he produced all kinds of material for tourists - postcards, guidebooks and so on -

meanwhile developing his own, more exciting history of his premises. Worth's lasted eighty years. Today's tourists will find an upmarket gift shop and the coffee house – called Tea on the Green – is next door, with windows changed to match Mol's.

Exeter's Guildhall (overleaf) is England's oldest civic building still in use. It has been the centre of law and order, as court house, prison, police station and site of the stocks, and the heart of local government. It was also a place of business, a meeting and feasting hall for the great and the good, a museum of municipal silver and other treasures, the focal point of the market, and the local water tower.

The frontage we see in our picture is still there but looking much newer, having been restored in 2009. It was constructed in the 1590s, although there had been guildhalls on the site previously. The columns are Dartmoor granite, and the portico resting heavily on the columns is Beer stone, like the cathedral's west front and, as with that monumental edifice, this was painted in bright colours too. The columns were gilded; such massive splendour in gold, cream, red and blue must have been eye-popping, and Pevsner thought it barbarous enough without the paint.

The prison cells are out of sight, in the cellars and at the back. Over the ground-floor cells there used to be a large water tank, supplying the citizens both free and otherwise, filled by aqueduct from the river Exe. Drips from it made life even more uncomfortable for those unfortunates below.

At the time of our picture, the room over the entrance was used as the council chamber, shortly to be reassigned as the mayor's parlour, and more lately as home to the more modest of the city's civic entertainments.

The Exeter Ship Canal was the result of a trade war between the port of Topsham, on the east bank of the Exe estuary, and the city itself, further upriver. A dastardly member of the local bigwigs, the de Courtenays, one Lady Isabella, Countess of Devon, blocked off the river north of Topsham with a weir, to gain water power for her mills (the locale is still called Countess Wear, spelled that way). Boats couldn't get to Exeter any more. Matters were improved in 1290, only for an even more dastardly de Courtenay to build another weir, so that ships had to dock at Topsham. Milord could then charge what he liked in tolls to permit transit of goods to and from the big city.

By the time a de Courtenay descendent, Henry of that ilk, had his head removed

by Henry VIII, Exeter could regain control of the river but it had silted up so wasn't navigable. The answer was a canal and by 1566 it was ready, under 3 miles long, 16 feet wide and 3 feet deep. It was never enough and only got going when it was made much bigger, but it did have locks (chamber or pound locks) on European lines, the first in England.

The Exeter-Topsham quarrel was finally resolved in 1676, when the canal was extended to that port, and later in its final version the canal was made 4 miles long and 10 feet deep, allowing quite big ships to use it, mainly pursuing the wool trade, pulled by horses along the tow-paths we can see.

It seems that our picture was taken from the Salmon Pool bridge, that now leads to the Double Locks pub, looking towards Exeter and the old Seage swing bridge, no longer there.

Numbers 78 and 79 Fore Street, Exeter, known collectively as Chevalier House, were Jacobean oak-framed buildings in which, despite local legend, Charles II did not hide after the battle of Worcester. By the early 1700s there was a pub here, the Fountain Tavern, later the Fountain Inn and the HQ of a wine and spirit merchant called Sercombe.

No. 78 was let in the mid 1800s to the mayor of Exeter, John Trehane, also a wine and spirit merchant, and he's still there in our picture, with Gunn and Burge's chemist's shop in No. 79. By 1929, they were selling apple juice in 78 and books in 79, but vandalism on an unprecedented scale was next door.

Woolworth's set out to buy Chevalier House, to demolish it and build a new and efficient threepence and sixpence store. The city fathers, aghast, borrowed some money and bought the building for the townsfolk, and let it to a publican as Ye Olde Chevalier Inne.

What Woolies couldn't do, the Luftwaffe could and the Chevalier disappeared along with much else in the bombing of May 1942.

If such a thing had happened in Delft, say, or Bruges, the Chevalier would have been rebuilt after the war, as it was.

As it is, those lovely Jacobean houses were replaced by one of the worst possible examples of 1950s' New Brutalist architecture you could ever see, anywhere. So, if you want to see what vandals can really do when they try, take this book and look across Fore Street at what passes now for the Chevalier Inn, and weep.

Our holidaymakers' wedding photograph, June 1901.

Acknowledgements

Many thanks for helpful information to Philip Hunt of Broadstairs; Christine Warren (see http://bbhilda.topcities.com/Folkestone/FolkestoneThen_Now.html); John Kenneth, The Eltham Society (theelthamsociety.org.uk); Stephen Bax (canterbury buildings.com); Colin at Lynmouth Museum; Alison Isaac (VisitIlfracombe.co.uk); John Howarth of Buxton; David Cornforth (ExeterMemories.co.uk).